SPARED

Chronicles of the Call:
Book Two

Marigold Cheshier

Firewind Ministries

SPARED: Chronicles of the Call: Book Two
By Marigold Cheshier

Firewind Ministries
1218 Oakhill Road
Ozark, MO 65721

ISBN: 978-1-939565-02-0

Copyright © 2016 by Marigold Cheshier
All rights reserved

DEDICATION

I dedicate this book to Max McGough, childhood buddy and lifelong friend, mentioned in the story *"Nosing Around."* He and his daughter, Michelle, traveled with us in crusades in Tanzania. Max, a defender of the faith, has been promoted to a better place called heaven.

I dedicate this volume to Wayne Rogers, a dear and trusted friend, who walked with us through the trauma of Mikey's burns. Wayne is among that great cloud of witnesses cheering us on from heaven's grandstand.

Most of all:
I dedicate this book to:
The Lion of the Tribe of Judah,
who has not, and will never fail us.

ACKNOWLEDGEMENTS

For reading my manuscripts with a critical eye and offering advice: Mike Cheshier, my husband of 50 years.

For great input and helping me to recall accurately some of our early adventures in Africa: Mikey Cheshier, our son.

For Mikey's written part in the telling of his story.

A special thanks:

To Lori Loomis for her constant source of encouragement and helping hands. How could I have gotten through the many other newsletters and correspondence without your help? I love you, Lori. You are a true woman of God. *(Contact: rogerandloriloomis@gmail.com)*

To Majetta Morris, my extraordinary editor, who knows just when I need a word of encouragement to keep me going. I couldn't have done this without you. *(Contact: Majetta Morris, Freelance Editor— Bright Light Editing, 3419 W. Camelot St., Springfield, MO 65807, 417-379-5596, majettamorris@yahoo.com.)*

To Steve McGuire who showed much patience as we struggled for an appropriate cover. *(Contact: Steve McGuire at McGuire Design Group for photography or design at 417-882-8673. www.mcguiredesign.net.)*

A very special thanks to you, the reader, and my friends, who have called, nudged, and pushed me to complete this difficult-to-write book. Without you, I would still be playing a tug of war over this emotional project.

I must say a reverent thanks to my sweet Jesus for helping me to write when I didn't think that I could write another word—when my vision was too blurred to see and my heart was broken. You, dear Lord, gave me the courage to push through the pain and complete the task for Your glory. I will forever be grateful. I could not have written a word without You. Thank You!!

I love you all,

Marigold Cheshier

TABLE OF CONTENTS

FOREWORD

SPARED FROM THE ORDINARY

Just to think about punching a clock causes me to hyperventilate. A routine lifestyle has never fit me very well. Evangelism suits me just fine— different locations, a variety of restaurants (I especially love local flavors), and meeting new people. I don't even mind a different bed every night as long as it is clean—free of bed bugs and creepy crawlies. If the bed is bad, then I'm excited for a change for sure. I hate filth as much as the most persnickety, fastidious little Suzy homemaker of them all, and recoil like an elephant gun at clutter. I do like to know what's on my floor. When traveling to new places my husband has had to look under the bed for me more than once. I like to keep my clothes in Ziploc bags, just in case a roach or something worse sneaks out of the drainpipe and decides to bed up in my clean clothes. I travel with a plastic mattress cover for those little emergencies such as the Tororo Guesthouse of Uganda.

When traveling between Kiasumu, Kenya, and Kampala, Uganda the Tororo Guesthouse is a spot in the road, a nightmarish caricature of a roadside accommodation. A short description of the accommodations is a thatched roof, dirt floors, filthy cots covered with dirty unwashed sheets, a torn pillow without a pillowcase, and a muddy-floored outhouse located off the grounds. If nature calls in the middle of the night, you must step over sleeping people on the narrow walkway in front of the few rooms offered to travelers, walk through the kitchen to make your way outside the "back door" into the dark night, walk down a grassy path, go through the flimsy gate, and continue walking through more grass until you finally arrive at the rickety, muddy-floored outhouse. It was, to say the least, quite the experience. However, that is another story for another time. Just let it suffice to say, the experience has been emblazoned into my memory.

All of these quirks were birthed in frontline battlefield tests that would have given most a diagnosable case of PTSD and persuaded them to seek another line of work. But through them, the Lord and I have hatched plans in the crucible of these experiences, which brought me much pleasure when they actually worked. Let me add, God's plans always worked; it is my concocted plans that actually make sense on paper but fail to produce the desired results.

I do get a thrill dashing into Wal-Mart shopping for an upcoming daring excursion of one sort or another; however, mundane shopping gives me a migraine. Day-to-day shopping trips are not my cup of tea. In other words, going to the mall or to the grocery store can be like a trip to the dentist unless I'm on a quest for something specific.

When God calls, He equips. At least in my case He has caused me to love the unknown, unexpected, and unpredictable life of a missionary evangelist.

I have found there are never two days alike in my life in the bush of Africa. The only thing I can count on is awaking to the chatter of the starlings, the mournful cooing of the doves, and the busy weaver birds as they greet the dawn by playing Catch-Me-if-You-Can on the top of my tent. Stepping outside is a breathtaking venture as I observe the Master Artist's combination of hues of the most magnificent colors across the canvas of the eastern sky. In the chill of the morning, I stand in awed silence at the Ccreator's handiwork.

The early evening brings back the cooing of the dove in its continual call to the world, demanding an audience, announcing that darkness is soon to arrive, and one had better make ready for the rapidly descending blanket of night.

Last, but not least, is the cacophony of sounds of the hyena's night song. If he has made a kill, he laughs a maniacal giggle to draw the other hyenas in the area, which is a survival tactic for this member of the mongoose family. He knows that if he doesn't sound this call, the others will smell the kill on him and they will devour him to eat the kill inside of his belly because he didn't alert them to the feast. Hey, it's the law of the jungle. If he's just prowling around, he hoots, shrills, cackles, and wails in a harsh discord of meaningless sounds—at least to the untrained ear. If he's quiet, he's stalking and hunting something; but you can be sure that he's there, just outside the light spilling from the camp lantern, hidden within the shadows of the squatty acacia. Whatever he's doing, he lulls me to sleep while listening for his sounds. Call it a false sense of security, but zipped up in my tent, nestled down in my clean sleeping bag, entertained by the night sounds, I feel as snug as a bug in a rug, and drift into a deep mindless sleep.

In my African bush world, there is no television, radio, or any such distractions; but rather a constant hassle of flat tires from the *kali* (bad tempered) roads, flash floods, or droughts, ministry in thorn ridden, harsh environment where food, water, and basic necessities for existence are only the beginning of the challenges. There simply wouldn't be time for inane trivia of the ilk of "as the stomach churns" or "love of strife" anyway. Just plain life is saga enough.

Exchanging the plush carpets of "the 'burbs" for nylon tent floors, the soft "ride like a dream" automobiles for rugged all-wheel-drive winching-yourself-up-a-mountainside beast, or preppy hip coffee shops with more choices than a Black Friday sale at Walmart or Dillard's for a boiled pot of java off the outdoor open pit fire served in a tin mug doesn't necessarily make me weird—just "SPARED FROM THE ORDINARY."

1

CHAINS, QUAGMIRES, AND NIGHT STALKERS

We could see it, even in the inky black of the African night, the unmistakable shape of a predator pacing up and down outside our vehicle, if you could call anything near an open-sided vehicle as being "outside." More than a windowless vehicle—it was like a jeep with plastic/canvas drops for windows.

We could not tell exactly what it was, but in the deep bush of Africa, it is almost always something dangerous. It seems everything eats, bites, stings, or hurts something or someone in some way.

A slow trickle of fear chilled my veins, which I immediately had to come against in the name of Jesus. The night had a million eyes looking squarely at us, or so it seemed. Hackles were at the ready—like soldiers on dress parade on my spine. I felt nauseous and it was all due to a lapse on my part. We had broken the number one axiom of driving decorum on the Dark Continent: never drive at night. It's times like this that as a believer I have to stand on the power of God to be my strength and courage, for there was a huge battle raging in the mind field.

It wasn't as if we planned a late night African safari. Forces outside our control had foisted this fear-filled evening upon us with the help of a 1974 Land Rover that refused to work as designed because it had long since passed its prime.

The adventure started earlier that day when the solid metal doors of the dank car lot creaked opened, and we drove the car off the sales compound into the formidable Nairobi traffic. Weaving through Nairobi traffic is an experience all of its own. If you are not a praying person, you soon learn how by thinking that every few minutes you stare a head-on collision in the face.

The truth of the matter was, originally we were scheduled to be in Eritrea, another East African country, not the bush of Kenya. On a Sunday one week before our departure date at Central Assembly of God in Springfield, Missouri, during the praise and worship time, we sensed God's presence. With hands uplifted, hearts open to receive from the Lord, we both felt strongly that God was telling us to change our tickets from Eritrea to Kenya. I will always be thankful for worship leaders like Tom Matrone who know how to step out of the way and allow the Spirit of the Lord to move on hungry hearts.

I leaned over and whispered in Mike's ear, "Honey, I feel God is warning us concerning

Eritrea. Maybe there is danger awaiting our team if we go there."

To my surprise, Mike said, "I feel the very same way."

When you're in the presence of God and He speaks something to your heart, you can *take it to the bank. It is as good as done!* We both knew on that Sunday that we would not go to Eritrea but to Kenya instead. God did not give us a reason; we just knew that we were to obey Him.

Blind obedience is tough.

I heard a story about a German Shepherd that hated the "O" word—obedience. His master decided he needed obedience school. It was tough for the Shepherd. When the master said, "Sit," he thought, "I don't want to sit; I want to go with you wherever you go."

"Stay," came the firm voice of the director.

"I need to find a fire hydrant; please don't ask me stay. I hate the 'O' word. Then the unmentionable happened, right in front of the poodle, I made a puddle. I was so ashamed. If it had not been for the 'O' word, I could have found a fire hydrant. That 'O' word gets me every time," said the German Shepherd.

Sometimes I feel a little like that Shepherd, when God says, "Do, go, stay," and I know not the reason why. But I know that I must obey.

Changing the flights for six passengers would not be an easy matter. We felt disappointment because our hearts were excited to minister in Eritrea; however, when God speaks we must obey, like it or not. Monday morning, I began negotiations with the airlines, and miraculously the company exchanged all our tickets from Eritrea to Kenya with no exchange fees required. Nothing short of a miracle!

When we arrived in Kenya, May 30, 2000, we learned the *why* of the softly spoken message from God to my heart concerning the change of venue. On the day originally scheduled to arrive, May 29, four Ethiopian MIG-23's fighter jets dropped bombs on the main airport in Asmara, Eritrea. God protected all of our lives without our knowing the awaiting danger.

Now here we were in Kenya, standing on the side of the road in the blistering hot sun, looking on helplessly as red mud boiled out of the radiator of our newly purchased 26-year-old African bush-weary Range Rover.

My mind drifted back to the early morning sequence of events when we had come to a decision that two hundred dollars per day to rent a car for three months is a monumental *chunk of change*. Mikey and I had set about to convince Mike, my cautious husband and Mikey's dad, that we should buy a used vehicle; after all, that would be cheaper in the long run, and be good stewardship of the monies God provided through wonderful people who believe in this ministry.

We knew that we needed a rugged vehicle for the bush that could take all the beating the African roads could dish out. Finding something that fit our budget, we discovered, was most laborious. In our search, we came upon a car lot that looked as though it had some choices we were looking for. There it was, a tough-looking, green Land Rover in all its freshly painted glory with the rust spots barely disguised and enough fiberglass bonds to build a speedboat, but it was in our budget. The front seats were bucket seats covered with a tough khaki-colored canvas. The second seat was a much too narrow to be comfortable bench covered with a brownish leatherette—a cloth that's made to look like real leather but is fake. In the very back of the vehicle were two small bench seats facing each other. The Rover was army green in color—inside and out. There was no padding on the roof or doors. No windows except for a drop canvas in case of rain. Everything was put together with nuts and bolts, not to mention some baling wire and zip ties. The demeanor of this vehicle said, "Bring on the African bush, I can handle it!" $6,000! What a deal. We disregarded the old saying, "If something is too good to be true, it probably is."

The dark-eyed, dark-haired, well-tanned owner, Heimy, an Australian living in Kenya, said, "Remember, Mike," and I quote, "at the end of the day, you want a Land Rover. It's the machine of Africa." I would live to regret those words as the future held for us a rude awakening, and we would soon be quoting the salesman's statement in contempt.

Heimy continued his pitch, "The radiator has just been cleaned, and the engine overhauled." That was a joke we did not yet realize. He convinced me with his next statement, "When the sun goes down in Africa, the vehicle that you want is a Land Rover" which, as it turned out, might have been true thirty years earlier. Those words cinched it for me, music to my ears. I could feel excitement bubbling in my spirit as Mike haggled over the price. I kept thinking of how much money we would save. We could build another bush church or pay the tuition of a few more students to EAST (East African School of Theology), if we bought rather than rented a vehicle.

"Come on Mike, let's buy this 1974 Land Rover. The dealer says it's in great shape. We are wasting our hard-earned money renting vehicles." Convincing Mike to change his mind on this idea of buying a used car was a bit like pulling a rotten tooth of a Cape buffalo, but after much twisting of Mike's reluctant arm, he relented.

We soon learned a valuable lesson: You don't want to take an old used vehicle to the bushland, for it could cost you your life. I can still hear Missionary Glenn Ford saying, "You really need a new, reliable vehicle; but if he really overhauled the engine, then you'll be okay." Thoroughly trusting—at that time, but not anymore—we believed Heimy. After much deliberation, we finally agreed on a price for the old girl. We paid Heimy and climbed into this green monster thinking we had really done something good. However, *at the end of the day* we found ourselves in the pit without the cherries to enjoy.

We had negotiated with a weasel with a nefarious agenda. In other words, he was as crooked as a snake on a rocky hillside. We should have picked up on this joker's real purpose when he told us he was moving his entire operation to Tanzania— probably in the dark of night. After a few hours of driving this vehicle we realized this man was a dirty dealing, cheating, deceitful, lying dog—and those were his good traits. This car had definitely not been driven by one little old lady and only on Sundays.

Navigating around the few vehicles remaining behind the stonewall fence, Mike eased out into the Nairobi traffic. I loved it. Finally, we were in a vehicle that could go the extra mile—a rough, tough, green machine. We loaded everyone and all the luggage into the green Rover.

Every thirty or forty miles we broke down for a multitude of reasons. The first three times I was sure that it was somehow Mike's fault—after all, this was a Land Rover much like the ones used in Tarzan movies. Who knows, maybe it had been a star in its day. When the radiator boiled out thick red mud, we knew that we had been *HAD*.

That's a terrible feeling: *being had*. I dealt with mixed emotions. I would have loved to kick Heimy in the shin right about then, but I had to demonstrate a sweet attitude—after all, we had guests. Oh, the things I would have loved to have said to that *junkyard crook*. Not only had he not cleaned the radiator, we also realized there had been no engine overhaul. Nothing he said was truth.

At dusky dark, we rolled into Narok, a humble Maasai town. There was nowhere to stay the night, and crunched up in the vehicle was an unacceptable option, so we continued the journey. While passing through Narok, Joseph Shikokoti, a dear friend and the fellowship pastor for Keekorok Lodge where we were headed to preach a revival, flagged us down. He notified the ranger station that we were delayed due to car problems, and would arrive after dark at the main entrance to the game park, which we had to go through to get to Keekorok. They acknowledged him and gave permission for us to travel at night, which is highly irregular due to poachers. (The Kenyan government takes serious offense of illegal hunters in the area, often shooting them on sight.) He assured us they would be watching for us and would alert the other game wardens that we had clearance. With that problem solved, Joseph joined us, and we continued our adventure.

Dark slowly descended upon us. We thought we had repaired anything that could go wrong with the vehicle, and the remainder of our safari would be eventless. However, there was one more sinister trap the enemy had devised for our destruction and intended death that lay ahead of us, having nothing to do with the old vehicle.

What's not to love about the African night sky unless the moon and stars have gone into hiding behind a blanket of black clouds? It so happened that this night of all nights was a moonless, starless black night. Traveling on such a night always gives me reason to pause. Anyone who is not at least slightly spooked might be *a few fries short of a happy meal,* or you could say *their elevator doesn't go up to the top floor,* but the exception to the rule regarding the fear factor is Mike and Mikey, my husband and son, who seem to thrive on adrenaline and laugh at fear— appearing to be unafraid of anything. Notice I said, "appearing."

The usual laughter, chatting, and singing inside the Rover—nicknamed "the beast"—helped to lighten the dark night that seemingly swallowed us whole. Essence of barnyard, zoo, and big game mingled with the distinct odor of cooking fires inside cow manure *bomas*—huts—from the village life of the Maasai drifted into the vehicle on dust-laden breezes coming through the open windows. These scents indicated we were getting deeper and deeper into the bush.

Seemingly like eons ago before we departed Nairobi, Mikey had purchased a heavy chain to secure the spare on top of the vehicle—which he had done with great excess, much to our auditory discomfort. The heavy chain link held the spare tire in place, leaving the oversupply lying on the metal roof. When asked why so much beyond the practical need, he replied, "God told me to."

"Mikey, I don't believe God told you to buy this much chain. I think it was the devil trying to torment us with the constant clang, clang, clang, while driving down these pothole roads."

This brought a chuckle from everyone. All was well in spite of the breakdowns we had endured.

"Mom, I'm telling you, God told me to buy this. Just you wait and see, we will need it for a very good reason. This chain might be a tool to save our lives."

Laughing, I said, "Come on son, I can hardly hear myself think. I can't fathom how this chain could benefit us." Another chuckle or two escaped my lips as we listened to the annoying chain clattering, jingling, clashing, and clanging.

There were a couple of very important people on this outreach mission with us—godly folks that I love and admire—Nicki Clausing, daughter of Diane and Ron Clausing; Denise Harrison, daughter of Wanda and Ron Harrison; and Cheryl Wood, a veteran on our trips. Diane, Wanda, and I were childhood buddies growing up together in the small paper mill town of Bastrop, Louisiana, where my mom and dad pastored for 27 years. They had entrusted their beautiful daughters to accompany and minister with us on the other side of the world. Nicki was a budding children's minister dedicating her life to the full time work of the Lord. Denise was studying to be a veterinarian. What a perfect place to learn more about wildlife, on Africa's plains! One more little detail that bears mentioning—Denise was three months pregnant with her first child. When I learned of her condition, I insisted she take the more comfortable seat in front by Mike. As things turned out, I'm not so sure that was the best choice. Remember she's never been to Africa before. Drivers in Kenya drive anywhere they jolly well want to—including the ditch, either side of the road, or wherever. If they are trying to miss a pothole, they'll play Russian roulette down to the last second.

It wasn't long until we were broken down on the side of the demolished road. I actually don't think it rated the name road, for the ditches were less traumatic than the supposed road, meaning we also preferred driving in the ditch. At times we had to get out of the ditch, and drive on the open ground to avoid collision with a driver from the opposite side of the road driving in our ditch. TIA—This Is Africa!

I wanted this trip to be a wonderfully memorable experience for everyone, especially these lovely young women. It definitely had started out being an unforgettable experience—as their worst nightmare—and I didn't see any hope of twitching my nose to make it different. We have another saying, AWA—Africa Wins Again!

Part of our regular equipment is flashlights. We try to bring the 5 D-cell magnum. Not only does it light up the world around you, and seems like it shines all the way to the stars, but it's a pretty good weapon if you find yourself in a situation where you need to waylay something or someone. Mikey was shining the light out the window. The green beast did not have glass windows, but rather a clear plastic drop tied at the top by a canvas strap, which when let down reminded you of looking through a gold fish tank. What I am describing is an open vehicle which doesn't leave you feeling very protected.

I did not dare tell the story of which we had recently become aware: while riding with his wife and young son in a game reserve, Kenya's top game officer was attacked by a lion. It grabbed the boy by the skull from between the unarmed mother and father, and dragged him out of the Land Rover, severely mauling him until, somehow, the father was able to reclaim his son.

I continued to push these concerns to the back of my mind, and kept up a jolly front. Glances at Joseph revealed that I was not the only one with a slight panic beginning to knock around my ribs. I noticed the whites of his eyes were growing larger—a little like neon lights on an old 50's style motel.

Calm down, Marigold, the beast is running better than it has all day and even though it's nearly

10:00 p.m., we're only a few miles from the game park gate, I kept reminding myself.

As we puttered along, I heard Mike say, "Son, turn that flashlight off: we might have a real emergency and need that light," with just a slight edge of concern, or was that genuine fear, in his voice.

"Really Dad! We just saw lions out there. We're having our own . . . *Night Safari*?" Mikey replied, with a little waver in his voice on the words *"night safari"* to indicate a fake tremble; but of course, he obeyed.

Some of the lodges outside the game reserve offer Night Safaris beginning around 9:30 p.m. until close to midnight at the cost of approximately $75 per person with the hopes of seeing bat-eared foxes, spring hare, white tail mongoose, and other nocturnal animals. On special occasions, night-hunting predators, such as lions or hyenas, are spotted. Although Mikey and the whole lot of us would have liked to continue searching for predators, respect demanded obedience thus giving up the chase. We had actually seen many beasts of prey— jackals, hyenas, and elephants—but we couldn't stop and take pictures for many obvious reasons—an open unreliable vehicle being the first one, and dark being another. Pictures taken late at night while driving are data stored in the memory bank of the brain with the eyes, and later retrieved to be replayed while daydreaming, or perhaps return as an unwelcome subconscious guest in your wildest, most frightening dreams—in other words, the stuff of nightmares.

I should lighten up a little. Why did I feel like something sinister was around the next bend in the road? Was it a premonition? Could it be that God was telling me to pray? You're a brave woman, Marigold, pull yourself together, I silently chided myself.

The clanging chain on top of the green can with wheels that we were told was a vehicle was only making matters worse. *Why did Mikey purchase that ridiculously noisy chain?* I felt a slow churning in my gut starting up as if I had just remembered leaving my curling iron on high in my empty house.

What was that in the middle of the road? It looked for all its worth like a river. Maybe we had taken the wrong road; but that wasn't possible since, as poor of an excuse for a road that it was, there was only one road to Sekenani gate—the entrance to the famous Maasai Mara Game Reserve. This infamous trail consisted of dirt, old broken tarmac, rocks of all sizes and shapes, and now the lights on our junkyard-refugee vehicle revealed a river directly in front of us. Being careful not to let the engine die, Mike gradually came to a halt to silently assess our predicament.

Panic shoved its fingers down my throat. *What will we do?* I said to myself. *This can't be happening.* I gasped.

A myriad of poor options forced themselves through Mike's brain and none were really good.

No one spoke a word for what seemed an eternity. It felt as if a thousand eyes were hungrily observing us—and every childhood monster from under the bed and in the closet were closing in for the kill. There seemed to be no sign of human presence for miles in any direction.

Uneasy thoughts of danger slowly trickled through my veins. *Lord, give us direction. Help Mike to know what to do,* I prayed.

Many cars had obviously driven right through the water, for their tire tracks led up the dirt incline on the other side.

"Okay, guys, we can't sit here all night, so say a prayer," Mike said as he shifted the Rover into first gear, and the wheels splashed into the water. Staring straight ahead, the dim headlights revealed a glimmer of rippling as we sliced through the dark, menacing hole. We sat on the edge of our seats hardly daring to breathe, quietly watching, and silently praying to make it to the other side.

Mike continued to drive.

With a controlled lightness in his voice he said, "Looks like we've made it. We're almost out."

Just as relief started to relax my nervous system, the surface under our left rear wheel disappeared, abruptly stopping the Rover. The left wheel churned water like the old waterwheel riverboat.

Now the mag flashlight was exactly what was needed.

Mikey climbed out of the vehicle for a reconnaissance of the situation. "Looks like there is a bottomless pit under this tire, Dad. Maybe you and I could physically lift the vehicle out."

Oh no! I knew what was coming next.

"Marigold, climb over the seat and take the wheel so Mikey and I can try our hand at lifting this car out of this pit."

"Mike," I protested, "I've not driven this car at all. I'm not familiar with the way it works, not the gears or anything about it."

"Don't fret! You're just going to stay behind the wheel and make sure the car doesn't die. . . . Simple."

I reluctantly clambered over the seat and slid into the driver's position so that I could put my foot on the gas pedal as he slid his off. Mike stepped out of the vehicle in nearly hip-deep water. I felt the caution rocketing through his veins. We had no way of knowing what else was in this water. I tried to settle into a comfortable position; my legs being much shorter than his, I could hardly reach the gas pedal.

Fear and resolve flashed across my inner man all at the same time. *I can do this, so why is there a sour taste budding in my mouth? Is it premonition that this is about to go south?* If I had only driven the Rover one time, I could possibly have gotten a feel for the beast. While riding in the back seat, I had paid no attention to the shift configuration; furthermore, the gear markings had long since worn off. The steering wheel was on the right side of the vehicle, making most things backwards to the USA.

Even though I grew up driving a big farm tractor on our family's 300-acre spread on the Bonne Idee Bayou in Louisiana, I was as nervous as a cat on a hot tin roof. "I can do this," I assured the passengers in a *sprechgesang* way. "Don't worry your pretty little heads; I've got this covered," I said with a slightly nervous chuckle, trying to reassure them—or trying to sell it to myself!

It's a good thing that people can only see your actions and listen to your words of encouragement; that they cannot see the struggle that goes on in the battleground of the mind or heart. I felt as if I was whistling past the graveyard, reminding myself that there was nothing to fear but fear itself. I shifted gears as Mike instructed, which required letting my foot off the gas pedal. As I quickly put my foot back on the gas in an effort to not let it die, I heard Mike say from the middle of the road where he was standing "DON'T . . . LEEETT . . . TTHEEE . . . CCAAARRR . . . DIEEEEE!!!!!!!!!!" With each word his tone went down in pitch, and the word die came out a slow, despondent defeat.

Oh no, no, no, no, not this. . . . Not now, Lord!—This can't be happening. I felt sick in my innermost gut. *What have I done?* Knowing the danger I had just put us in caused a flash of terror to rattle my chest. My heart panged. *This has to be a nightmare . . . only a bad dream. Surely I'll wake up from this terrible predicament and say, "Whew, it was just a bad dream."* But it was not just a bad dream! It was a reality! I had made a terrible mistake! I felt nauseous!

I should have never taken my foot off the gas; how was I to know? I gasped. *How could I have been so stupid! Please, Lord, let this dumb car start!* I turned the key. Nothing . . . nothing but the soft click of the key in the ignition acknowledging my futile effort. The headlights, taillights, and what few dashlights there were on the Rover plunged into blackness. The silence was deafening. No one spoke or moved for what seemed an eternity. The blanket of night closed in around us immediately.

As I crawled back over the seat, I had to push down the terror trying to boil up in my being. I was embarrassed, angry with myself, and concerned for all our safety. The moon and stars buried behind a curtain of clouds made it difficult to see even your own hand in front of you. We were all at least slightly unnerved as anyone stranded in a seasonal river while trekking across Kenya in the dead of night would be.

Dripping wet from waist down, my husband resumed his place in the driver's seat. He never blamed me or even rebuked me—at least not with words or actions. He just sat there. Helpless. He didn't have to say anything to me; I was saying plenty to myself. The blame was squarely on my shoulders. I reasoned with myself, *If I had just driven the old beast for even a mile, I could have surely been able to handle this simple request.*

How hard is it to keep the pedal pressed down so the gas stream remains constant?

Mikey stood watch on top of the car by shining his magnum light in every direction, looking for wild animals approaching. As he made a sweeping arc, the beam of the mag light completed a full circle. Its illumination revealed attentive unblinking eyes glowing toward our helplessly buried vehicle.

Liquid seeped under the doors. We were stranded in water slightly deeper than our floorboard. Knowing what lives in these flooded area creeks gave me reason to be anxious. I began to scrutinize the floor beneath my feet, for I knew that snakes were not just a real possibility, but more like a likely incident. There are fast and aggressive black mambas, green mambas not as aggressive but just as deadly, spitting cobras, puff adders, and many more species. The water drives the snakes out of their death dens.

Snakes were not our only concern. *Dear God, what have I done?* The thoughts of our danger made my heart race and my chest tight.

"Mikey, come inside the car, Son. I have an uneasy feeling," I said.

Without windows there's very little protection, but at least it's better than standing on top of this

Rover, making yourself a target to the larger animals such as a leopard or lion that would not hesitate in one effortless leap to join Mikey on top of the vehicle for a midnight snack—he being the snack—I thought.

A lion can actually stretch twelve feet without having to force a leap. I have a snapshot I took in the Aitong area of a lioness high in a tree escaping a herd of Cape buffalo, so I know for a fact that lions can climb trees. Leaping to the top of our little car would be a piece of cake for a lion. Knowing that lions roamed this very stretch of road after dark did nothing for my nerves.

Leopards were also a possibility. A leopard can lie for hours without moving a muscle, just waiting for the right moment to pounce upon its unsuspecting victim with blinding speed. His feet are steely muscles with claws designed to gut its prey while its fangs go for the neck and jugular veins. Killing is quicker than you could say scat. We were stranded in big cat territory where leopards regularly roam day and night.

Let's not forget the elephants that live in the area. Elephants attacked and killed cows at this very spot, and would not hesitate to charge our little measly group. In addition, don't disregard the hyenas and packs of wild dogs.

Although it is hard to comprehend that our lives were actually in danger of being a meal for a hungry lion, a stalking leopard, an angry elephant, or a slithering snake, the real truth is that any of these scenarios were a real possibility.

I'm so grateful that our son is obedient. Mikey slipped his wet body into the car beside me. Nicki sat on my left, then Joseph Shikokoti. We were packed like sardines, which actually yielded a little comfort. Possibly we would look like too big of a blob to tackle instead of many small portions.

Joseph Shikokoti said, "Everybody! Shhhhh! Don't make any noise. This is bad, really bad. Don't talk, be quiet."

An inexplicable feeling swept through my stomach when my eyes adjusted to the darkness just enough to see the fear written on his face. He lived here. He knew the real danger that we were in. The intonation in his voice spelled terror. Fear is catching—like telling a scary story to a gathering of little girls at a pajama party, and listening to their squeals. I resisted the panic that tried to put a hook in my insides.

It seemed impossible that just a week before I was worshipping God in church, hands raised, with no threat to life unless someone broke into my home in the middle of the night to do me bodily harm, or I pulled out in front of a semi on my way home from shopping, but I wasn't in America the beautiful. I was in the bush of Africa, stranded in water, in lion country with no visible way to rescue myself.

No village campfires were seen in any direction. We were like sitting ducks just waiting for calamity to strike. Wafting on the air were the scents of wild beasts nearby. Could it be an elephant or a herd of elephants? The minutes drifted in and out, as darkness tried to gobble us up. The occasional lunatic calls of the hyenas sent chills down my spine. Perhaps they were headed to our waterhole for a drink—not a comforting thought.

Something paced back and forth some twenty feet to the right of us just on the other side of the water's edge. Hyenas smell like rotting flesh—blood and bones. Their odor is so stout that it has at times awakened me out of a deep sleep. I thought, *I wish we knew what was there, but it's probably just as well that I don't.* We didn't shine the light to see what it was. We needed the precious batteries. We had to trust God to protect us no matter what danger awaited.

Mikey wanted to walk the mile or so to the gate. Of course I was dead set against it—it wasn't even an option—no, absolutely not! It would have been disaster looking for a place to happen.

Leaning forward, I whispered in Denise's ear, "Are you afraid?" I could see the trickle of tears rolling down her cheeks as she just nodded, yes, too shook to speak. It didn't take a rocket scientist to accept the fact that we should all feel a measure of fear; I certainly did but dared not admit it. Ever trying to be the comforting one, I said, "Don't worry. It will be okay." However, I knew we were clearly in a dangerously compromising predicament.

As I leaned back against my son's extended arm, he could feel my body shivering—partly from the damp coolness of the night, and partly trepidation. Now it was his turn to whisper in my ear. So softly no one could hear he said, "Mom, you are trembling. Are you cold, or are you frightened?"

I whispered back, "Yes on all accounts. We are in serious trouble."

In a chiding tone, he simply said, "Mom."

I felt ashamed to reveal the raw feelings of fear to my brave son. I know that the spirit of fear is not from God, but from the enemy of our soul. It brought a pang of remorse to admit such weakness to myself. I needed strength and courage to face this situation. Knowing where my strength lies, I began to silently pray, "Lord, take my fear away. I know that You do not give us the spirit of fear, but of power, a sound mind, and love. Fill me with Your power. Give me a sound mind and strength—Your strength."

As I silently prayed, I felt God touch me, washing away the fear and trepidation. I quietly raised my hands toward heaven in the darkened car in worship of the Great I AM. I began to pray softly at first as tears tumbled down my cheeks, and each tear shed brought with it freedom from fear, and a swelling of internal victory. Soon I could no longer hold back the praises exploding in my spirit. I burst forth with a booming voice, praying in the Spirit, "Let every man and beast hear me and join in, but I cannot sit quiet any longer." There was a fire shut up in my bones that demanded release. My heart burned within me in the presence of God.

For the next several hours, I prayed—without restraint of voice—in the Spirit, refusing to give place to the outside noises or movement surrounding our vehicle. I feel for sure that I spoke in key lion and key Maasai giving explicit instructions not to eat or harm us.

About three-thirty in the morning, I ceased praying, knowing in my heart the danger had passed. It was the darkest hour of the night. There were no stars or moon. We had sat in this watery pit since 10:30 p.m. We could not even see our own hand in front of our face, but I knew the danger was over, and my heart could feel the bright of day in spite of the pitch darkness. I felt we could all get out of the vehicle for the trouble was over, the storm had passed.

For the next few minutes, we sat silently basking in the presence and peace of God. Then to our amazement, headlights appeared on the hill to the left of us. We were no longer alone. How odd because there was no road there; but we watched as a large lorry—truck—slowly made its way down the hill and onto the very road where we were. We held our breath as the lorry hesitated when it reached the road more than a half-mile away. We focused on the headlights and sounds to determine the direction he would choose to go. With no lights working on our vehicle, the driver had no way of knowing that we sat stranded and in need of help. Sound travels a long distance at night in Africa. It is said that you can hear a lion's roar five miles away during the night.

I heard the lorry driver bring the gear to first, and watched as the headlights beamed toward us. *Yes, praise the Lord, he's coming our way. Thank You, Jesus. You have heard our prayer.*

As the lorry rounded the bend in the road, and started down the slope toward the waterhole, his lights revealed an old green Land Rover blocking the middle of the road—us. The lorry wheel chassis was much higher than ours. He could have driven right through the river and made it. But there was no way he could pass us on either side, for we were slap dab in the middle of the road with zero shoulder.

At first, I thought that maybe he was an angel sent by God to rescue us out of our dilemma; however, he was drinking. I still felt that God led him to help us.

After the introductions, the men tried to find something with which he could pull us out. But he had nothing. All we had was the chain on top of the Rover that God had told Mikey to buy! He climbed on top of the Land Rover, and retrieved the chain lying in the middle of the spare tire.

The chain exactly reached from one vehicle to the other except for something to connect the ends of the chain together. Need is the mother of invention. We had a need. What could be used? We have a hasp given to us by a state trooper for protection. If opened all the way, and the small end placed into a link of the opposite end of the chain, then the hasp could hold the chain together.

It worked except for one small detail—someone had to hold it in place. Mikey, with one foot on our car and one foot on the truck, held the chain together with the hasp. Had the chain been one link shorter, it would not have worked. It was evident that God had spoken to Mikey about buying a chain. A niggle of concern plagued my heart for my son's safety, but he quickly shushed me. To the best of my ability, I quelled the thoughts of disaster. There was dead silence inside the Rover. I think I forgot to breathe.

The lorry driver put his truck in reverse, and slowly eased up the steep embankment backwards. The tires inched through the water and, in a few short minutes, the Rover pulled free of its quagmire, and eked up the steep bank as the lorry continued its backward haul. With every rotation of the tires, my heart grew more excited. With eager anticipation, I wanted to break out singing to the duo vehicles the nursery song about the little train that could, "You can do it. You can do it."

Finally, upon reaching the crest of the slope, the chains were disconnected. The Rover immediately started a speedy backwards descent, back toward the water. Seconds before we landed smack-dab back into the middle of the water hole, Mike popped the clutch, and the engine came to life. I realized he had purposely allowed the car to speed backwards so the popped clutch would jump-start the engine, and it worked! Mike put the Rover in first, and we climbed back up the hill on our own continence.

I leaned back against the seat and let out my breath. No one was eaten, bitten, or stung during the nerve-wrenching ordeal.

Africa will stretch you beyond what you think you can be stretched. It will trample not just your last nerve, but every nerve you have and those you didn't know you had. It can be unforgiving, relentless, and deadly—or make you think you're going to die. If you really want to know a person, spend a few weeks in the bush of Africa with no running water, no toilets, electricity, or modern conveniences. It even gets better if you get caught in an unexpected monsoon rain that lasts for days, keeping you from rolling up tents or getting out. The rich dirt turns slick as glass when it's wet.

This group had proved their ability to endure whatever was thrown at them.

In a short few minutes, we arrived at the game park gate. The wardens had been very worried for us. They had expected us at 10:00 p.m. and it was now 4:00 a.m. They gave us the clearance to drive on to beautiful Keekarok Lodge where we had reservations. About 5:30 a.m., we arrived safe and sound despite all the trouble.

Joseph looked at me and said, "This is a sign from God that no animal nor man can touch you or bring you harm. You are here on divine appointment, and God is your Protector."

After checking in at the front desk, we were taken to our small A-framed individual cottages—barely large enough for a bed and bath—one of about twelve units facing the drive. Behind the units were heavy bushes with the space of about fifty yards, and then the workers' quarters. There were no fences. The lodge, the oldest in Kenya, was built in the middle of Maasai Mara Game Reserve. It was not unusual to see elephants or a pride of lions walking through. Vervet monkeys and baboons were everywhere, but it still felt like civilization. There was a dining hall and patio to view the animals and gorgeous grounds.

Finally in our room, you would think we would fall across the bed and sleep—that long-awaited rest from the harrowing previous night. All I wanted was to shower the filth that felt inches thick from my body. The shower was awesome. Luxuries like showers in the bush of Africa after a night like the one we had just experienced are breathtakingly fabulous.

By 7:30 a.m., I strolled outside our bungalow, praising God that we were all alive, present, and accounted for. I noticed a native in full Maasai dress, greeted him in Kimaasiai, and realized he could speak English. I said jokingly, "Where were you when we needed you last night?"

Without batting an eye, he asked, "Were you in the green Land Rover on the main road in?"

I said, "Yes, that was us."

He just turned and walked away with no answer.

Within a few hours, Joseph let us know that some thieving Maasai had purposely dug the hole—well-hidden by the water—in the middle of the road to trap unsuspecting travelers after dark when there was no one to see their scheme of robbery. Several fell victim. No one laid a hand on us. The Maasai saw us, watched our every move, but held back from doing us bodily harm or simple robbery by God's protecting power. Joseph called it right when he said, "No animal or man will touch you or harm you."

We held a crusade in the afternoon and evening at Keekorok Lodge, and ministered in the morning at the neighboring villages just outside the park—including the one that had schemed to ambush us. Many came to the saving knowledge of God.

We now have a church at that very village, birthed from the harrowing experience of being stranded all night in hip deep water. It's in times like this that we are made keenly aware of God's watchful care. I have learned that He will never ask one of His children to do what He does not divinely equip you to do and make a way for His purpose to be accomplished.

2

GOD SENT A WART HOG

We sat around a crackling campfire on the bank of the Mara River in the famed and storied Maasai Mara Game Reserve, sipping hot tea or coffee, and listening to the wonderful backdrop of night sounds—hippos snorting, the ever nervously wary and apprehensive zebras sharply barking, and a pair of lions roaring in the distance—as we planned our one-day game drive starting the next morning. We were completely oblivious to the fact that we were drawing attention to our excited, happy band of gospel crusaders until a couple from England eased up beside me and introduced themselves, after which she said in her heavy British accent, "Don't get too excited about seeing lions. This is our third trip to Kenya, and we have yet to see the first lion."

"Oh my," I said, "the lions and I have our own thing going. If you want to see lions, come with our team, and you'll see them," I said with great confidence bolstered by many years of successful experience.

I must have made a believer of her as she responded, "We have a professional safari van and driver; will you guys ride with us?"

We turned to our team and asked, "Do you mind if we ride with this couple tomorrow when we go out on safari? They haven't seen any lions, and I'd like to help them locate a few before they return home."

They all agreed that it was fine.

At first light the following day, we pushed off after a predawn cup of hot coffee and cookies. If we were lucky, we would catch lions on a hunt or maybe even with a kill, and return to the safari lodge for a late breakfast.

The morning was crisp and alive with the songbirds making merry music. The hyenas' hideous laugh, the lions' roar, and all the unidentified sounds of the African night had diminished. Only the beauty of the morning remained. Danger from any four-footed beast seemed to be a tale told around campfires, and not really a reality at all. How could any place so beautiful be a threat?

Hunched against the cutting cool morning wind, we were wrapped in our red checkered Maasai blankets—the official wear of the storied warriors—to protect ourselves from the chilled air produced by the ex-celebrated dizzying speed of perhaps ten miles per hour of the open Land Rover. It's all a matter of perspective, you know.

We were moving along a game trail that spidered off into many directions. After driving approximately an hour, the cool morning quickly began turning hot. We drove through hay-colored short grass—which also happens to be the color of lions—with the open plains on the left, and rows of thick bushes on our right.

Mike began to have rumblings in the stomach signaling the oft-repeated case of diarrhea—we call it Jomo Kenyatta's revenge—which is a part of his life in Africa. We have time and again laughingly said that if Mike ever has the opposite problem back in America, all that he has to do is look at a map of Africa! Problem solved!

As we continued the safari, his abdominal discomfort became far more urgent until he had no choice but to ask the driver to pull over so that he could relieve the insistent pressure exploding like a thunderstorm inside of him. The driver made several circles in the grass—looking a bit like a carousel at a carnival—to make sure there were no lions hidden there. Feeling convinced that Mike would be safe, he dropped him by a small acacia tree and drove fifty yards away.

Just as Mike assumed the position for this form of business, seven full-grown healthy hungry lionesses—apparently having missed their last night's kill—shot up out of the grass from different directions, which we thought was clear, and headed straight toward Mike. He was the undisputed center of their Pavlovian attention. These lions had hit the jackpot. Now there are no words to express how one might feel in such a delicate position as stalking lions that come calling with the intention of having you for their mid-morning snack. Things had looked brighter for Mike. If you would not be just a little concerned, then your elevator doesn't go all the way to the top floor.

We cranked up the Rover to run interference and pick him up. It was all happening so fast. I was terrified that this would be the day—doomsday— for my brave honey. "God, do something," escaped trembling lips.

Out from the bushes came a warthog running for all it was worth, squealing to the top of its piggy voice. It looked as if it was running in the Swine Olympics. This commotion caused the attention of the lions to remove their amber hungry eyes from Mike. The chase began to see who could catch the warthog first. One of the lions flipped the warthog over. The prey appeared to be getting away, but the hunter as quick as lightning circled back and nailed the bugger. All seven lions entered the eating frenzy of their catch—while it was still alive I might add—not giving it the dignity of killing it first.

Obviously, Mike's life was spared, and the English couple's wish fulfilled: to see lions. None of us bargained for such an up close and personal encounter with the king of the jungle. Our team, not far behind us, caught the whole thing on video. Mike was at the mercy of God, and He knew just what dinner menu would distract the lionesses.

This was not the first encounter we had experienced with warthogs. While spending the night at Keekorok Lodge, we heard a loud scream from Bob and Ruby Hoke's room. A warthog (who incidentally was named "Pork Chop") weighing about 200 pounds had leisurely ambled into their room. When it walked into the bathroom, Ruby closed the door and screamed for help. The swine intruder was trapped in the bathroom. The terrified animal was wailing and shrieking an alarming high-pitched sound of panic, which could have easily broken a glass, and made a soprano at the Met jealous. I'm not sure who screamed the loudest, Ruby or the warthog. With the help of Mike and Moses Sayo, our dear friend and fellow warrior for Christ, standing on the rim of the tub—not wanting to risk the fury of the unhappy hog's tusk in their extremities—kicking and poking it with the end of an umbrella in the tush for several minutes, it was finally driven out of Ruby's bathroom and house.

This same warthog that resided for a while at Keekorok—one of our favorite stops on a hot day when traveling through that area—noticed that our young grandsons, Michael and Maurice, were being surrounded by several large baboons. Pork Chop, the name lovingly given to this seemingly resident warthog, put herself between the boys and the baboons. One by one Pork Chop chased them away.

Later, on a subsequent trip to Keekorok, we asked where Pork Chop was, for she had become a fixture to us, and we missed her. Never getting a straight answer, we were suspicious that she had become part of the chef's special. We really hated for such a wonderful pig to disappear, but in truth, she was delicious. If that evening's pork special was indeed Pork Chop, then she entered the ministry with grace and dignity. Pork Chop had a reputation for attacking people or things that she did not like or by which she felt threatened.

We will forever be grateful for the warthog that drew the attention of the lions that saved Mike's life, and our good friend, Pork Chop, who saved us in other ways.

3

MONKEY BUSINESS

Out of nowhere, I felt the sharp canines like barbed wire penetrate deep into the flesh of my upper thigh as the unthinkable happened. I squealed, wrinkled my face in pain, and grabbed my leg. Jumping back, I saw the flea-infested mangy miscreant—a large vervet monkey— skittering away like lightning into the dense thickets surrounding us. The nasty little bugger is known to carry all kinds of diseases on its filth-laden teeth; and it had just left me with four holes in my leg. In my wildest dreams, I would never have anticipated being bitten by anything larger than a pesky, malaria-ridden mosquito. I had dropped my guard for only a moment; but in Africa, a moment is all it takes for the unspeakable to happen. I had allowed myself to become distracted by taking photos for one of our guests to add to his memorabilia of an African experience. The lighting was perfectly without glare due to the heavy rain clouds forming overhead. The acrid, musty odors of scat and urine mixed together permeated the pre-rain air as a lucid reminder that we were "not in Kansas, Toto." Perhaps this caused the animal to become so aggressive. Or it could have just been due to the fact that the armed guards who usually sat under a tree at this locality on the famous Mara River had vacated early to prevent being trapped by the rains that were obviously on the way, and the vervet felt free to do as it wished. However, there remained the third possibility that sent a quiver down my spine: the monkey could have been rabid.

The days leading up to this dreadful monkey incident had been filled with successful ministry. We had conducted crusades in the cities, as well as made long treks deep in the bushland to primitive villages along the animal trails and tracks someone dared to call roads. We were allowed to visit schools during assemblies to share the good news that Jesus saves, and were given the opportunity by headmasters to give to every child a Bible in his own language. Oh, for those opportunities to return to our land.

Everyone was quite tired from the rigors of these forays into territories that Satan thought he owned. In fact, some were so tired that a few chose to stay at the procured tented camp accommodations and rest rather than to go on a guided camera-safari hoping to see African animals such as the famous "Big Five" creatures like the magnificent elephant or "His Majesty, Ole Simba," himself.

Mike had remained at the camp with those needing rest, and I had taken the team on the game drive. Dual leadership has great advantages.

Personally, I can't imagine such a decision to stay behind. How could one possibly miss being stuck in a slimy mud hole out on the savanna; or having his olfactory senses blasted with the aroma of dust and dying grass through the open windows; or being chased backward by an angry charging elephant with one monstrous tusk holding you responsible for his dental problems. Not to mention the possibility of gazing into a male lion's eyes where you can see your reflection laid out on his table next to the mashed potatoes and gravy with an apple in your mouth. Oh yes, the *Simba*— the lion's Swahili name—often caresses the van with his thick black mane, checking it out and causing you to freeze, stop b-r-e-a-t-h-i-n-g, and feel an invigorating surge of adrenalin. The adventurer in me won't allow me to lag behind and sip coffee or tea. No way!!! There is just too much to experience out there. There will be time for front porch swings, sipping tea, and eating cake in another life.

After bringing many people and leading many such excursions, we know; and knowing that not everyone is wired like us, we do try to be sympathetic to the limitations and desires of those who are working side-by-side with us. When we feel that a team is worn out, we try to plan a break in the schedule to relax and regroup; it is critically important. Our team members come from cities all across the United States, and vary in ages and occupations. The one thing that brings us together is reaching the lost with the gospel of Jesus Christ. The team needed this day of R&R, and it had been wonderful up to this point. This was the last hurrah, an afternoon of camera safari in the reserve before heading back to a more civilized area of Kenya.

We had seen just about everything there was to see in the game park, but the safari was quickly about to go south. It had taken most of the day to arrive at our destination—the Mara River in the Maasai Mara Game Reserve. This bend in the river is the home of families of hippos, large crocodiles, occasional elephants, baboons and monkeys, and animal sign—such as tracks and scat (poop to the uninitiated) from lions and other equally dangerous critters hanging around during the night and early morning, and any creature in the reserve that chooses to roam here. Vervet monkeys have particularly claimed it as their hangout, habitat, turf.

This place is popular because it is one of the only places in the reserve that allows tourists to get out of their cars, walk around, and indulge in photo ops of the indigenous animals in their habitat. If brave enough, a picnic can even be arranged—near the open door of their vehicle, if smart.

Most Americans visualize hippos as cute, round pink toys wearing frilly skirts, and monkeys as pets sitting sweetly on the shoulder like Tarzan's buddy, but this could not be further from the truth. The wild life of the bush country of Africa will bite, scratch, claw, eat, or sting you in a heartbeat. Everything and everybody is somewhere on the food chain. The exotic animals of Africa are definitely a matter to be reckoned with.

The game wardens had posted guards dressed in khaki green military attire and outfitted with AK47 assault weapons since a hippo incident a few years earlier at this very spot. A vanload of tourists had gotten out of their vehicle to take pictures of the crocodiles and hippos in the Mara River. One of the tourists, a young girl about twelve years of age, walked through the brush at the top of the river bank, and came face-to-face with a startled hippo who instantly killed her with sword-like teeth powered by strong massive jaws.

The hippo is responsible for more human fatalities in Africa than any other herbivore (plant-eating) animal. Male hippos actively defend their territories, which run along the banks of rivers and lakes. Females have also been known to get extremely aggressive if sensing anyone coming between them and their babies, which stay in the water while she feeds on the shore. Hippos have been clocked at speeds of over thirty miles an hour—easily outrunning a human—and have enormous jaws hosting up to twenty-inch canines. They weigh between one-and-a-half to three tons (1,500 to 6,000 pounds). The hippopotamus, one of the most aggressive creatures in the world, ranks among the greats of Africa's deadliest animals: hippo, lion, crocodile, mosquito, black mamba, great white shark, buffalo, elephant, and puff adder.

However, to my misfortune, guards were nowhere in sight on this day.

After a long bumpy journey, making one feel like a ball in a pinball machine, we had finally arrived at the famous river. The bank gradually sloped down to the water's edge in some areas, but in others there was more than a ten-foot sheer drop created by erosion of the mixed sand-and-buckshot mud banks to the water's edge. You could see the crocodile slides from the top of the bank into the water, and the trail the hippos used for their evening wanderings, which can be as much as thirty miles in a night as they forage for food. It takes a lot of green plants to fill a three-ton body. It was oddly quiet, much too deserted for my liking, when I exited the van. The gentle breeze rustled through the squatty myrtle bushes with not a guard in sight. Not even one? Where could they be? What's up with this? My first thought was to look around for fresh lion tracks. Possibly the guards were forced into hiding due to a pride's—a group of lions—appearance. A strange indefinable wariness began to creep into my mind. A vague warning sounded off in my thoughts accompanied by a twitching in my stomach. I hate it when that happens; it always signals trouble. I cautioned everyone of the pending danger, pointing out the absence of guards.

"This could mean that lions are about, so don't wander into the bushes. Stay close to the van. We'll leave all the doors open just in case. Don't get too close to the water's edge; and this is not the time for inner reflections, so don't walk off alone," I said.

I would have liked to have said, "We're not getting out," but this was the only opportunity this team had to take photos of the hippos leisurely frolicking in the famous Mara River, and for many years before the killing, there had been no guards here. The game park approved the stop for exiting vehicles and even picnicking. Reluctantly I quieted the voice in my head. "It's okay," I said to myself. But I was not doing a great job of convincing myself that all was well.

When we had started out about 6:00 a.m., there had not been a cloud in the sky. Often in the savanna where one can see for miles, the thunder rolls and the sky blackens with no rain resulting, but that would not be the case today. We wasted no time taking photos and eating a few snacks. I was still fighting this mind-troubling uneasiness—like danger was there and I just couldn't see it. The blackening sky warned of possible bad weather moving in.

"I think it's time to vacate this place. Did you all get some good shots?" I asked.

"Just a couple of more shots before we leave," John said.

I replied, "Would you like for me to take them so that you can be in it as well?"

"That would be great, thank you."

Most of the group stood by the van waiting to get aboard and continue our safari. There were a few small vervet monkeys playing rather close by that would make an interesting photo—one that really would speak of Africa.

John had a first class camera with large telephoto lenses so that when I brought it to my eyes to focus on him and the kiddies, I was blinded to activity going on around me. I held his Canon camera up to my eye, and manually focused for the best shot possible. The Mara River infested with hippos and crocs was directly behind me, and to my left some fifty feet away was heavy thicket. Our van was about thirty feet away on my right; and beyond the van, the land opened up to the savanna.

The large vervet monkey ran out of the thicket from my left straight for me, circled me, and slapped my skirt, all of which I was completely unaware because the camera was plastered against my face. When I didn't move, it ran up my leg, stopped mid-thigh, and planted its vicious, no-nonsense bite. As quick as it bit, it ran back into the thicket, leaving me reeling in shock of the whole ordeal. It all happened so fast! Thank God, it didn't come all the way to my face.

Everyone insisted we discontinue the safari, and head back to camp. I strongly rejected the notion, saying, "It's just a monkey bite." In my heart, I knew the danger of such a bite, but I really didn't want to disrupt the group's safari on my account. If only we had been in our car instead of a rented van, a medical kit for road emergencies would have been available.

Some of our ministry during the previous days had included medical, and I knew supplies were completely diminished. As I climbed into my second-row seat of the van, my eyes immediately settled on a large red medical duffel bag on the seat beside me—previously it had not been there. This was the first of a long list of miracles surrounding this story. I was shocked to see it sitting there. Maybe I had somehow missed it; however, not likely, as during the long hours of safariing, I had repeatedly changed places in the van to get the best view for my camera, and to rummage around for snacks and drinks. No, absolutely not; I had not missed it. It was my personal medical kit, big as life perched by my seat as if it had been summoned from the trunk of our car to this rented van by my wishing it was there. How could it be? The hand of God was already revealing His power and presence. The joy of discovering the medical bag dwindled as the realization hit me that I'd used all the medicines in this bag, and there was zilch for wound care left. We had had so many wounds in the clinic, I clearly remember emptying the contents of the Betadine, peroxide, and alcohol. However, I peeped inside to see if there was anything I could use to clean the wound. I unzipped the bag and was amazed to see a brand new unopened bottle of Betadine with a pointed tip on the end, and new unopened packages of sterile gauze, as well as sterile gloves—just what I needed to clean the nasty wound. I quickly opened the Betadine, and unscrewed the cap on the pointed tip. The smell of antiseptic wafted across my senses. With the sterile gauze in my gloved hand, I forced open the first deep puncture wound from the monkey's teeth, and filled the hole with the golden brown liquid. Using the gauze pad, I massaged my skin and pressed the medicine as deep as possible, then moved on to the next wound. Feeling slightly queasy from the self-inflicted pain, I made the rounds to each wound the four teeth had made, pressing and massaging.

The rain dropped heavy and hard as if feeling my trauma. I'm reminded of a song I sang when I was a young girl of ten or so about God's big tears being rain. Soon what seemed like a simple cloudburst progressed into a seriously unrelenting storm. First the heavy rains caused instant mudslides for the vehicles on the open plains; and then, the hail pounded like machine gun fire from the prince of the powers of the air and his cronies. Yes, unbelievable as it seems, large hail poured down from the heavens in sub-Saharan Africa. On the other hand, perhaps it was God punishing the monkey who dared to bite me. But I have to admit, it was uncertain exactly who felt the punishment the hardest—me or the monkey.

Conventional wisdom suggested the safari was over, and to head back to camp. On a clear day with no stopping for animal photo shoots from where we were in the Mara, we would be four hours from the Sekenani gate, plus another thirty minutes on a dirt cow path road to the Siana Springs tented camp where the remainder of the team and my sweetheart, Mike, awaited.

After about fifteen minutes of kneading and poking the four tender bite holes, my head reeled, nausea churned waves within my gut, my hands sweated beads like an athlete under pressure to win the prize, and I knew there was a real possibility I was going to pass out on the dirt-laden van floor. Surrendering to the fact the safari was a wrap, with weak voice, I instructed the driver to go to Keekorok Lodge located in the middle of the park where I was well acquainted with the doctor who manned a small clinic for the staff.

Everyone, with the exception of my nauseated self, was enthralled with the mud ride created by the incessant hard-driving rain and hail on mud paths. It reminded me of the song "Slip Sliding Away," as the icy rain pelted down upon us. Most things in life remind me of a song; and if one has not already been written then I'll just pen one for the occasion.

Everyone was a bit giddy from the fishtailing of the van on the soaked mud track. Hail, occasionally mingling with the hard-driving rain, did not slack up. My head continued to reel, and my stomach threatened to lose its contents. What a wimp I'd turned out to be!

After what seemed an eternity, we arrived at Keekorok Lodge—possibly the most famous of the game lodges in all of Africa. We had passed many vehicles stronger and better equipped than ours to weather such a furious storm. They were stuck up to their axles—completely stranded until the storm passed, and help arrived to rescue them. Leaving them in our wake, we dared not try to stop and help as we ourselves were at times sliding sideways or backwards, but still moving nonetheless.

The staff workers for Keekorok Lodge, who knew me well, came to the van with a large umbrella and helped me out. We had preached many revivals for the workers back in the workers' quarters. The rain pelted us like pea gravel driven by tornado-like winds as we made our way to the doctor's quarters. However, much to my dismay, no one was there. After further inquiry, we learned the doctor had left early that morning and would not return for a couple of days. My staff friends at Keekorok were deeply concerned as due to the language barrier, they thought a serpent had bitten me. We now had no choice but to continue the difficult journey to our tented camp, which was still several hours away. The roads became more difficult to navigate with the continuing inclement weather. The rain continued pouring in proverbial sheets, causing all the seasonal rivers to rise out of their banks.

Our driver, Steven, clearly traumatized by my monkey bite, was very disturbed about the entire incident.

We came to a seasonal creek turned raging river. The four-wheel-drive tourist Land Cruisers were backed up in convoy about seven cars deep refusing to cross, thus preventing the rest of us from doing so. Steven rolled down his window and commanded all the other drivers to move, saying, "I have a life to save." I thought that was a bit overly dramatic.

The other drivers said, "It can't be done; none of us can cross those raging waters until the river goes down some. It's entirely too deep and treacherous."

He replied, "I'm going through one way or the other."

I said, "Steven, why the rush? We will wait like the other vehicles until it is safe to cross."

He said, "My best friend was bitten by a vervet monkey, and we could not get him to a hospital in time to begin the rabies series, and he died of rabies. I don't want that to happen to you."

I sat back pondering his statement as Steven passed one vehicle after another, approaching the river.

I said, "Maybe we should wait with the others."

However, his determined face was set like a flint to the other side of the river, literally come hell or high water. Conviction, single-mindedness, and purposefulness clearly was his driving force. In his mind, he was saving my life—and who knows, maybe he did.

Meanwhile back at our camp, Mike nervously sat under a large acacia tree near the dining tent as his spirit warned him something was badly wrong. Mike reposed on a stump cut for a seat next to the fire pit filled with cold ashes, which at night was ablaze and party to many wonderful camp-appropriate activities. While ruminating the possible causes of his sense of disquiet, Mike looked toward the entrance to the facility. There he saw me walking through the bush wearing the same dress I had worn that morning, and carrying an umbrella. I passed in and out of sight of Mike's vantage point. Because of the direction I was taking, he knew I would follow the path, which would take me behind and past a big tree, and into the open. He quickly made me a cup of coffee in hopes to warm me from the chilling rain. However, I never arrived at the tree! Mike's joy turned to puzzlement. So he got up and went to see why I had stopped behind the big acacia. I was not there! Where on earth had I gone so suddenly?

The apparition was so real that Mike began to ask various camp staff if they had seen me. For a good twenty minutes, Mike looked in every nook and cranny of the familiar place before it finally dawned on his mind; it was time to do some serious praying. With a now-cold cup of coffee in his hand, he began to pray for my safety.

Steven managed to pass the caravan on the mud-ridden trail; and now we stared straight at the water as he mentally maneuvered his plan of action. I swallowed hard as he said, "Hold on, everyone," and eased the van into the deep water. Our wheels completely submerged, and water splashed high up on the door. The odor of muddy manure-tainted river water filled our nostrils, but Steven kept going. Our wheels slowly turned, churning the muck and sludge; but surprisingly, we rolled out of the river and up the embankment, slinging the slush from all four tires. To the onlookers' amazement, we had successfully navigated the raging current, and were safely on the other side. We could not slow down, or the mud would cement us in place. As I peered back over my shoulder, although we had been successful, no one else attempted the crossing.

Slipping and sliding, we continued the journey toward Siana Springs.

SianaSprings in the local Maasai language means *the plentiful springs*. It is truly an area of abundance in flora, fauna, and Maasai culture. The camp has a rich history dating back to 1920, when the first game warden selected its current site for his camp. We first stayed there in 1982, shortly after it had been a hunting camp in the 1970s. The camp is now located on a wildlife conservancy, and is truly a magnificent place. An amazing forest of lush palms and indigenous plants thrives from springs and rainwater percolating down from the Ngama Hills. There is a stunning array of massifs lining the conservancy.

The streams and rivulets with fresh, clean water flowing through this area are home to a denizen of forest animals like the earth-colored bushbuck, tree hyrax, and the colobus monkeys that reside at Siana Springs Camp. Normally elusive and only occasionally seen in the wild, the bushbuck stroll in through the camp, not shying away from us. In the wild, these beautiful antelopes keep alert for the predators that stalk the savanna, and flee at the first sign of danger, making it difficult to see them up close and personal. The tree hyrax, a tree-climbing rodent-like animal, is related to the elephant—not in size but in the structure of its dental and feet alignment. Nocturnal, it spends most of the day resting in the hollows of the trees, easily seen at close quarters by your tent. On the high canopies of the acacia and other indigenous trees at the camp, it's fun to observe the resident troops of the increasingly rare colobus monkeys leaping from branch to branch foraging for leaves. The colobus monkey is arboreal, and seldom comes down to earth; unlike the pesky vervet monkey that had just taken a piece of my flesh, and steals the sugar and bread from your table. One vervet ran off with my cup of hot coffee in hand. I must admit they are comical. When I was overnighting at Keekorok, two of them opened my door, stole, and devoured an entire box of anti-diarrhea medicine. I laughed so hard that I cried. The vervet monkey that bit me was neither comical nor cute; this was no laughing matter.

Leaving the muddy roads, we traveled an indigenous gravel bed road that twisted and turned toward the camp. The green painted gate nestled into the thick bush line that surrounded the camp was a beautiful sight indeed. Peace, tranquility, safety, and a feeling of arriving at home swept over me. The air was crisp and clean smelling from the heavy rains. It continued to rain, but not nearly as hard. I let out a sigh of relief. When the gatekeeper swung open the gate, much to my surprise, Mike was waiting in the rain at the gate with the guards.

The first words out of his mouth were: "What happened?"

I said, "What makes you think something happened?"

My mind flashed back a few years earlier to an incident when a man in our church, who later turned out to be a charlatan, gave me a new red 300 ZX car, and Mike a powder-puff blue Lincoln town car. Filled with excitement, I immediately drove it to my friend's house to show it off. When I returned home and pulled back into our driveway, Mike was standing there with his hands on his hips. I pulled up and said, "What?"

He simply said, "How fast were you driving?"

I felt like a schoolgirl who had just been caught skipping class. I laughed a nervous giggle and said, "A hundred-fifteen miles per hour."

Mike said, "The cars go back today; we will not accept such extravagant gifts."

I said, "How did you know I was speeding?"

He replied, "I don't know; I just knew." That was the last of the beautiful apple red ZX.

Now, he just knew again that I was in trouble!

"Because I know!! I saw you under an umbrella, and discovering that you were not here, I knew something was terribly wrong."

"Okay," I said. "I was bitten by a vervet monkey. It's really no big deal." But in my heart, I knew better. I wanted to keep up a brave front for the team.

There was a small infirmary for the workers at Siana Springs camp. A young man with no medical credentials, but who wore a lab coat, said, "When did you have your last tetanus shot?"

" Well . . . uh . . . It's been more years than I can remember," I finally replied.

"You must get to Nairobi to a doctor, and start the rabies series of shots. I will give you a tetanus right now; then you must go immediately to Nairobi," he said with more alarm than I felt necessary.

I said, "There is no way that I can go to Nairobi until tomorrow. We have a team that has paid to be here in the game park, and I simply won't cut their time short."

Why does it always seem things have to be so difficult? There is always a tradeoff. Bad things never happen at a convenient time.

Tenacity prevailed as I argued much of the evening with Mike. The only option was for the entire team to leave the park, drive late into the night, and check into a hotel in Nairobi with no reservation where there was no guarantee of getting one room, much less ten rooms. There was no extra vehicle, so it seemed cut and dried to me: WAIT!!! It seemed the only plausible answer.

The danger in waiting had to do with the issue of rabies or blood poisoning from the filmy residue on the teeth of the critter that carries so many diseases. The wild monkeys of Africa carry most of the diseases that are dangerous to humans, including the tuberculosis organism. There are other dangerous diseases monkeys can transmit to people like yellow fever, falciparum malaria, Kyasanur Forest disease, Tanapox, and Mayaro virus. Some of the diseases depend on mosquitoes, ticks, and biting flies to transmit from monkeys to humans. I was excited to discover—fortunately for me—leprosy has never been reported to be transmitted from infected monkeys to humans. However, there are cases of zoonosis, whatever that is. There is even some suspicion that the AIDS virus originated with monkeys.

Most of these diseases are spread through a bite or exposure to the saliva of monkeys, or their nasal secretions. The rest are spread through exposure to monkey feces. Well, now, I had the bite, saliva, and possible nasal secretions; the jury was still out on the monkey feces. I wanted to laugh out loud or cry; I just wasn't sure which emotion I should allow to burst forth, so I just sat there stunned, saying very little.

Monkeys are subject to sudden and violent mood swings—particularly those with identity issues. A monkey peacefully grooming or playing can, without warning, attack. Monkeys also have a strict pecking order. Sometimes their attacks are attempts to assert themselves in their perceived pecking order. I have often wondered whom my monkey was trying to impress. Fearful monkeys also bite to defend themselves. But hey, I didn't even know this monkey existed; he came out of nowhere—so there must have been a pecking order thing going on in the bushes. As far as the rabies issue goes, if you wait too long to start the injections, then it can be curtains. These are the things I was being told. We prayed, pondered them, and then—WE WAITED!!!!!!!

It was the only sensible thing to do.

During the night, my leg throbbed at the bite site, and I couldn't help but wonder what sinister disease was working its malice into my blood stream.

About 7:00 a.m., we gathered in the camp dining area for breakfast.

The dining area—hued from canvas, native stone, and logs—is a work of art. The tables are carved from heavy split logs, covered with acrylic, and polished to perfection. The back wall is made of tightly constructed canvas stretched between foot-thick round log beams. The wall on the left side—constructed of stone and logs—leads into the kitchen. The right wall is made of only about three-foot tall logs and canvas. The front is a completely open courtyard, with specially cut stumps encircling the fire pit. In the evening, one of the camp workers entertained with melodies from *The Lion King*, jungle songs, and Kenyan ballads as he sang and played his guitar by the fire's glow under the stars. It was just a little piece of heaven.

However, on this early morning we had one goal in mind—pack, eat, pay the bill, and get to Nairobi. The chef stood with skillet in hand behind a table laden with a small burner ready to prepare our breakfast order. The table in front of him was lined with eggs, onions, tomatoes, peppers, and cheeses for omelets; or pancake batter to concoct sweet crepes with homespun condiments such as chocolate, homemade jams, or fruit. There was coffee, tea, mango juice, passion fruit juice, and tropical fruit juice. Slices of pineapple, pawpaws, oranges, and watermelon were invitingly arranged next to the juices. There were homemade breads and crescent rolls with specialty jams. We hurriedly enjoyed our breakfast. Mike paid the tab and loaded the vehicles before I could turn around good. As fast as lightning, the whole team headed to Nairobi—still sticking with our original schedule, but more hastily.

We tracked over the dirt roads of the game park area, and began the long, arduous journey. It was past lunchtime when we arrived on the outskirts of Nairobi, and everyone, except me, was hungry. We pulled into the Java House, which has American-type food featuring hamburgers, fries, and milkshakes of more flavors than Sonic, such as real mango and other local fruits. When the group was seated, Mike asked Bob Hoke to take care of them until we returned, and Mike and I left for Gertrude's hospital to see Dr. Nesbit, a children's doctor that I had seen on other occasions.

As usual, his office was busy. The smell of hospital mingled with baby odors and children at play met me when I opened the door. It did not matter to me that I was too old to qualify to see my doctor friend right now. I felt like a little child needing a little sympathy time after being bullied on the playground. Toys, books, and various items used to entertain the younger set while they nervously waited their time with the doctor were scattered around. I was concerned the team would finish eating before I could enter and exit.

I jumped just a little when the nurse called my name in her Kenyan-English accent, and followed her down the hall to the last door on the right to Dr. Nesbit's office, thankful that Mike was with me. Upon examination of the wound, Dr. Nesbit said, "Ordinarily I would reopen and scrape the wound to prevent blood poisoning, but you have thoroughly kept the wound clean. What did you have to use out in the bush?"

I proudly answered, "Betadine and sterile gauze. It was miraculous how I came to have it. I wouldn't let the wound close up," I bragged, feeling somewhat like a schoolgirl who had just received an A on her final exam.

"You may have just saved your own life," Dr. Nesbit replied.

My mind thought back to the miracle of the first aid kit being in the vehicle, and I knew the One who had saved me wasn't I. Seventeen hours had passed since that crazy monkey had attacked me.

While the good doctor turned his back to me, fiddling with something on the counter, he said,

"We must start the rabies series. It should have been started immediately, and seventeen hours have already passed."

Taking on yet another feeling, one of adult reticence, I said, "I can't take a live serum because I've had cancer. I've been instructed never to take live serums, so the shots are out of the question for me."

Without missing a beat, he turned, injected the needle in my flesh, and slowly injected the thick syrup. While administering the inoculation, he explained that there is no cure for rabies, and, if the monkey had rabies, without this series of shots, I would die. If too much time elapsed, the shots would have no effect. Again, he stressed the point, "There is no cure for rabies. If you have been infected; then you will die, simple as that."

It didn't matter that I was a cancer survivor and shouldn't have a live serum. The rabies was now the immediate threat to my life. There was no choice. The rabies trumped the cancer card.

Not happy with the way things had turned out, I shook Dr. Nesbit's hand, paid my bill, and made an appointment for my next injection. The driver returned Mike and me to the Java House to reunite with the team. They had long since finished and were awaiting my news. I shared all my happenings, and we then proceeded to the Utalii Hotel. I never ate; I wasn't in the mood.

Checking a large group into a hotel in Africa is always an organized chaos—everyone's passport copied, checked, and forms filled out. After a forever time, you are given keys, and porters start the process of taking the bags to the rooms on the one small elevator that stops mid-flight when the electricity goes out—which is every day, several times a day. Often I opt to climb the stairs, which is a better health preference anyway.

Within a couple of hours, I noticed I was seeing double, and, by evening, I was seeing triple. Fever, chills, vomiting, joint pain, and severe weakness captivated my body. I tried to sleep, but was tormented by the nightmares. The shot site was swollen, itching, red, and painful. I developed a monstrous headache, and dizziness ruled my every move. Muscle pain, nausea, and unrelenting harsh stomach pain gripped my abdomen. The injection had made me quite ill to say the least. If I weren't dying before the shot, I certainly was now.

The next day Mike took me back to Dr. Nesbit, and was sure the injections would be stopped since I was experiencing such violent reactions . . . or was it the rabies disease working on my body from that crazed monkey bite? Why did that monkey choose me to attack out of all the hundreds of tourists that stop there? I must wear a sign that says to mosquitoes and small critters, "Bite me, I'm juicy!"

The doctor insisted I must take all the shots in the series, just as directed, and the symptoms treated as they came. By the end of two weeks, the symptoms had subsided just in time for another shot. Once again, within a few hours after the injection, the whole ordeal started again! With each injection, my body was taken prisoner and tormented, only releasing its bars just before the next injection. Who could have ever dreamed that one common green monkey, better known as a vervet monkey, could wreak such havoc on one little missionary—but it did. After fighting the effects of the shots for more than three weeks, we felt I should fly home and have Adam, our son-in-law who is a surgical PA, administer the remaining three weeks of injections.

Sleep eluded me because of the pain in my body. When I did happen to drift away into the land of so-called bliss, it was everything but euphoria. I would find myself in the bush lands of Africa, surrounded by elephants, with no visible means of transportation, trying desperately to plan a way of escape. This dream often rolled into another terrifying dream of lions stalking me, in which I experienced feelings of helplessness and stark fear. At other times, there were both lions and elephants—always with no way of escape, no one to protect me, and nowhere to go. I would wake in a cold sweat just before I was devoured or trampled to death.

I finished all the shots, and gradually began to regain my strength. Two months later, I returned to Africa. In the deepest part of my heart, there was a trickle of trepidation that I would be terrified of the monkeys and any unprotected situation I might find myself.

The first week in country, I walked down an obscure path in Maralal, a remote area of northern Kenya, and an entire family—about ten vervet monkeys—stepped out of the bushes onto the path, heading straight for me. Without giving it a thought, I looked them straight in the eye and said, "Come on! Make my day! You take a bite out of me, and I'm biting back!" The monkeys jumped up, out of the way, and ran like scalded dogs. I laughed out loud, realizing that I was as tough as ever—maybe even a little more hard-bitten than before.

4

NOSING AROUND

My throat tightened like a hunter stringing his bow. My lips trembled, tears filled my eyes, and I had that sick feeling of faintness crashing in on me. The minutes drifted in and out. My heart beat so hard it shook my body. Breath backed up in my throat.

"Marigold, hold the flashlight steady and right on the nose so I can see where to place the stitches."

"I'm trying." I couldn't keep my mind from drifting like clouds on a breezy summer day to thoughts of the weeks before this moment.

At the request of the Assemblies of God director of Tanzania, we had been targeting the Kigoma area in western Tanzania with outdoor crusade meetings to plant new churches in hard-to-reach areas. Kigoma is a lake port town in western Tanzania, on the eastern shore of Lake Tanganyika, and close to the border with Burundi. It serves as the capital for the surrounding Kigoma Region with a population of 135,234, at an elevation of 775 meters.

Max McGough, a pastor at the time, and his daughter, Michelle, a talented music director, had joined us in this ministry. The combination proved to be most successful. Michelle and I sang with Max often joining us during our performances. Our voices blended very well. Max played his horns—a saxophone and a trumpet—enrapturing the audience as they soaked up the sounds like thirsty sponges. Being an accomplished musician, he switched between the instruments, pleasing the crowd, and drawing many guests to the crusade. Mike and Max did most of the preaching, but I altered in occasionally. Many came to the Lord. We give God all the glory for the successful church plant.

Now we were all very tired, but it was a good tired—one you feel at the end of the day when the house is cleaned, clothes are washed and put away, dinner dishes are back in the cabinets, and the place is spotless. Now that's a good tired! And it speaks of accomplishment.

The return journey had been a long one of nearly three days. We had crossed the great Serengeti plains to get from one side of Tanzania to the other. The road from the Serengeti to Kigoma was dirty, rocky, and horrible. The road with deep holes looked like it had undergone bombing runs from malevolent warplanes. It's funny how you remember the dusty, bumpy roads when you can't remember anything else. Kigoma roads were some of the worst we had ever experienced, and, after all our years of African ministry, that is saying something! Michelle and I bounced as rag dolls riding an old-fashioned Conestoga wagon.

Finally, we arrived at the Tarengire tented camp— a nice overnight stop before crossing the border into Kenya. It consists of a few tents sitting on top of a ridge looking a bit like a row of vultures sitting on the edge of a cliff watching for prey in the valley below. The back of the tent unzipped into a small bathroom with walls about four to five feet in height with perhaps two feet of space to the thatched roof above, which would be nothing for most dangerous African creatures or predators to slither or crawl through. Nightly trips to the "powder room" were quite the experience, and not for the faint of heart. I half expected to come face to face with a lioness or leopard while taking care of business in the appropriate "open" cubiclel. Let's talk about feeling vulnerable!

Mike, exhausted from the expedition, felt a little exercise might work off some of the tension from the day's rigorous drive. He dropped to the tent floor and began to do push-ups in rapid repetition, forgetting that he had a concealed ten-inch knife hanging around his neck under his clothes. He had removed his shirt for his exercises, but disregarded the dangerous knife. He had completed more than twenty push-ups when a downward thrust caused the knife to catch between the floor and Mike's nose. The point caught the floor, and his nose hit the butt of the knife, causing the cartilage of the flared part of one of his nostrils to tear loose from his face. Blood poured profusely from the wound. We applied pressure but his flesh hung, but we couldn't stop the bleeding.

We were not just hours, but maybe days from medical assistance. I finally walked up to reception to see if per chance any medical personnel were on the premises, though in my heart I knew better. I ran into one of our missionaries who was escorting across Tanzania a medical team with a lady doctor. They were checking in to the lodge for the evening. After a quick introduction, I explained our situation to her. She said she had no medical supplies left as her ministry time was over. However, on a whim she opened her oversized purse, and began digging like a dog after a bone. Much to her own surprise, she found a needle, surgical thread, and numbing medicine: all needed for the procedure to put Mike's nose back together—no more, no less.

She came to our tent to examine Mike's wound. "Another fifteen minutes and the tissue would have begun to die, complicating any cosmetic surgery. We need to do this now," she said. "When you get back to the States, you can have it re-cut, and a plastic surgeon can make it look much better." We never followed through with that advice. We didn't have to.

"Marigold, hold the beam of the flashlight directly on his nose, and steady," the doctor ordered.

It's amazing to me how strong we think we are until put to the test. "Sure!" I said, "Absolutely!" I said. "I've got the light taken care of."

However, as my attention came to the needle that she intended to use to reconnect my sweetheart's nose to his face, my tough demeanor vanished. I thought to myself, *How will this lady see to stitch up Mike's wounded nose if I faint?* I have to admit at that moment fainting seemed inevitable.

The sun had bedded for another night, and the only light we had for this delicate surgical procedure was this flashlight in my hands—and they were getting less steady minute by minute. I felt the blackness begin to envelop my brain like black clouds moving inexorably closer as a thunderstorm, trying to disconnect me from the events, and making good on a threat to drop me to the floor. Nausea caused my hands to sweat as I watched the needle plunge home—right into Mike's face—pulling the thread through and into the nostril. Again and again, the doctor skillfully drove the needle into the bleeding flesh. I couldn't look away; it was critical for the flashlight to remain steadily on the spot. Slightly swaying, feeling very faint, I watched my husband being sutured in a tent—a makeshift operation room at best—in the Tarengire Game Reserve in Tanzania. I willed myself to continue holding the light, but my stiff upper lip was wavering.

A familiar, kind voice broke into my thoughts. It was Max. As Max reached out and took the flashlight from my shaking hand, he said, "Why don't you let a man hold this light?" He could see the pallor of my skin, and probably suspected I was on the verge of fainting.

Not wanting to appear the wimp that I felt I was at this moment in time—especially in front of my suffering husband—I simply replied, "Thank you, Max, but really I could have continued. However, I'm sure you can hold the light steadier than me."

In my secret heart, I will forever be grateful to my lifelong friend for coming to my rescue—or should I say Mike's rescue. It was easier to sit on the floor beside Mike, and show my sympathy with "oohs," "aahs," and "ayes," while, without being obvious, looking away from the stitching.

Mike's biggest concern was the lions in the area. We have seen and heard lions in this place early in the morning, afternoon, and during the night. They pretty much roam around these tents as they wish, which, given my love for the furry beasts, makes it one of our favorite places to stop when crossing from one side of Tanzania to the other. But if they caught the scent of fresh blood in the air, and cast their amber eyes through slits in the tent on his very white hide, then they very likely could come ripping through this small tent with their monstrous claws like knives cutting through soft butter, and devour us all. We didn't even have our two bodyguards—viz., Smith and Wesson—as firearms are illegal.

It was at this very tent—our favorite by request because of its distant location from the reception—that a lioness swaggered right in front of us in broad open daylight. The high curved escarpment where the tents sit offers a spectacular view of the valley below. There is a nice stretch between each tent which makes this last tent—the one we prefer—appear to stand alone. Mike and I enjoy the seclusion even though the dining area is quite a distance away. The Tarengire Reserve is small in size, but more than five thousand elephants claim it as home. So, it's not unusual for elephants to drop by as well. We love this little tented camp because of its lack of modern conveniences, its rustic atmosphere, and its purely African ways.

On a different occasion, in 1995, we had concluded a successful crusade with over 11,000 people a night in attendance in Dar Es Salaam, Tanzania. Hundreds, if not thousands, came to the saving knowledge of Jesus. We had dared the impossible, a production of the "Heaven's Gates—Hell's Flames" drama. Forty-four American team members joined us in this great undertaking. Let me just say that much can be accomplished for the kingdom if you do not care who gets the credit. I am a team player; I really believe in group ministry. We brought all the stage props from America, which was quite expensive. We incorporated Tanzanian nationals to play the speaking parts. What began as a forty-minute production resulted in a three-hour production due to the embellishing of their acting roles. The Tanzanians did an incredible job with their acting responsibilities, and the crowds ate it up.

Michael and Maurice, our grandsons, made their debut as the dynamic duo singing the Rich Mullins' great song, "Our God Is an Awesome God." In their four-year-old pronunciation, they sang, "Wen he's wollin' up his sleeve, he's not pooten on da witz." How very cute they were, each insisting on his own individual microphone. Definitely, the crowd loved them. After singing, they climbed on top of the missionary's Land Cruiser and viewed the crusade—a safe place to avoid being crushed, or worse, by the mass exodus at the conclusion of the drama.

After the crusade ended and the teams returned to the States, we drove from Tanzania to Kenya, making a short stop at the Tarengire Game Reserve. As we were traveling through the reserve, elephants began to chase us. For a moment, I had apprehensive thoughts as to whether we would escape without harm because of the huge sand bed in a dry riverbed slowing our escape from the charging elephants. I turned to the twins to make light of the situation. Trying to keep them from becoming afraid, I said, "Boys, how did you like that?"

We were astonished by the *big boy* reply from such a little one as Maurice said, "I am horrified!"

With that I said, "Would you boys like to go back to the camp and color? I believe I have coloring books and crayons as well. We'll get a soda and just have fun."

With big smiles, they said, "Yes, that sounds like fun."

Mike headed back to the tented camp and dropped us off. I bought us a coke and snack, and we walked the long distance back to the tent. We sat on the porch of the tent, coloring, just enjoying the afternoon. Michael knocked over his coke, and the bottle shattered. He was so embarrassed that he began to cry. I said, "That's why they call it an accident. Nanna will have this cleaned up so quick that it will make your head swim." I started singing, "This is the way we clean up our mess" to the tune of "Let's go 'round the mulberry bush."

As I swept and sang, I heard rustling in the bushes in front of the tent. I stopped dead in my tracks. A frightened guinea fowl squawked and took flight. My heart stood still as I heard the low guttural growl of the lioness. This was not good. I had two four-year-old boys with a lioness in the bushes just in front of us. I quickly grabbed the boys and ducked into the tent. The windows were unzipped, leaving mere mesh walls. We huddled on the floor under the window out of sight, but not out of the smell of the predator. Barely allowing myself to breathe while keeping the boys perfectly still and silent, I listened for any movement to indicate what the lioness' next move would be.

The next few moments seemed like hours. I could barely make out the movement when the lioness sauntered on down the path just out of sight. It seemed like an eternity that we stayed huddled under the mesh window.

When we felt the coast was clear, we left the tent and walked toward the dining hall—the same direction that the lion had walked—so we could be around others and hopefully some guards. When we arrived at reception, guests were standing on the edge of the escarpment viewing a lioness that had just walked up and stopped to rest some fifty yards below. It was the same lioness that had passed by our tent only moments before. Thank God, she was not craving two young boys and a grandma for her afternoon tea.

Mike had reason for his concern over lions. They were most certainly around.

5

OF MUD AND MINISTRY

In the famed Loita Hills of south central Kenya, with the backdrop of all the rich night sounds of the African bush, from the zany whoop of the ever-present hyena to the distant complaints of the deep voiced lion, we discussed our operation plans for the next mission outreach. After much discussion, we decided on the mountain segment of the Maasai, known as the Dorobo. We had not been to this tribe, but had heard they were hungry to hear the *good news* of salvation.

After returning to Narok, the largest town in the district where we work, we embarked on a kidney-thumping, spine-numbing drive on a terrible *Kali*—Kiswahili for fierce—road. Some of the straight-up climbs on dirt paths were intimidating, but doable. Bob, Ruby, and John Hoke, plus Bill Howard were our team members. The Dorobo tribesman walked in front of our vehicle, leading the way to the area where we wanted to camp and work. There was no sign of a road or that one had ever existed.

With his long doubled-edged machete, the local guide hacked at the thick bushes to clear a path. Many times, Mike used a shovel to build up a washed-out embankment to make it passable for the four-wheel-drive bush vehicle. After seemingly an eternity, we finally reached the area to set up camp. The Dorobo backwoods bushmen were more accessible from the campsite located on the edge of the small escarpment with a small flowing stream.

After a short time of our sojourn, dark clouds rolled in indicating yet another heavy rain was imminent. The continuous roar of thunder sounded much like an angry lion with a bad case of heartburn. The clouds tumbled noisily about the skies—clapping as if praising God or scolding man, clapping and roaring such that you could hardly hear yourself think. Flashes of lightning zipped across the skies, lighting up the very corner of our limited universe. Then came the rain—heavy curtains of rain filling all the ditches—threatening to inundate our little camp.

Our camp perched on the edge of a small ravine with a seasonal stream. In the evening we gathered the water from the river for our baths. We had tried the solar bags that lay in the sun for a warmer shower, but the water was so muddy and stinky, we could hardly stand to use it even for our sweat-soaked, dust-covered, nasty bodies. Mike discovered a three-foot round by four-foot deep hole of water on the crest of a small hill where the cows came to drink—and do nature's business, he discovered by the resulting squish between his toes. None of that for me! I quickly decided that baby wipes would do me very well, thank you; and on this trip, that wasn't even a hard decision.

One morning before the rains set in, our good, long-time friend, Bill Howard, took a stroll to explore a bit. While negotiating a slippery, winding trail in the nearby forest, his feet slipped out from under him, and he careened down the embankment, making the song "Slip, Sliding Away" take on a whole new meaning. Fortunately, Mike was about halfway down to help him stop before too damaged. Bill was a muddy mess, and remembered where he had to clean up.

One of our forays for ministry required negotiating an approximately twenty-five-degree incline of rain-drenched forest. It began by crossing a swollen river at the bottom of the mountain. Then the slippery, sloppy, mud-hindered effort continued by slinging mud and sliding from one side to the other of the self-made road of the seemingly straight-up incline. Mike worked the four-wheel drive for all it was worth. I hung on for dear life and prayed aloud. The engine whined and the wheels struggled for traction as mud completely covered the windshield.

It would not have been a pretty scene had we tumbled down the mountainside with a carload of passengers. Above the noise, in a desperately demanding tone, Mike said, "Open your eyes and turn my windshield wipers on! I can't let go of the wheel!" By the grace of God, we managed to make it to the top and our camp.

Each trip out became increasingly harder as the unseasonable rain came every day. More than once, we slid into a ditch. Mike could barely stand as he connected our winch to a tree. Of course, I wanted to help. When my feet made contact with the slippery red-clay mud, they skidded out from under me. Fortunately, I had not let go of the door handle. Realizing my uselessness, I hoisted my muddy self back into the vehicle, and left it to the men—after all, God made them for such tasks. The old winch bolted to the front of our vehicle came through, pulling us the remainder of the way after hooking, pulling, and hooking again and again up the steep embankment away from the lurking river below.

The rains made ministry nearly impossible. Every day about two o'clock, they came with a fury and continued throughout the night. We ministered in the morning hours since that was the only break from them at all.

Then getting across the river when the time came to leave became a concern. Additionally, packing our wet tents would ruin them. They were to be stored at the General Superintendent's church compound in Nairobi, so they had to be dried, packed, and ready for storage upon arrival. We began by taking one down each day to dry them out. The last night there were only two tents remaining for all of us. It was an interesting night as all the guys slept in one, and all the girls slept in the other.

The next morning, we set out for Narok. We were more like a sled than a car as on some of the inclines we slid rather than rolled down the mountainside. We crossed the swollen river just "by the hair of our chinny, chin, chin" of Three Little Pigs' fame, but God is truly good, and His grace is sufficient.

Many came to the saving knowledge of the Lord Jesus Christ, making all the mud battles worthwhile. A church was birthed out of those challenges.

6

MAASAI MIRACLE

As we began another soul-safari into virgin territory, as far as the gospel is concerned, the arid and parched trail twisted through miles of increasingly formidable country. A few squatty acacia trees speckled the terrain. Once again we were seeking unreached areas to preach the word of God with hopes of salvations that would lead to a new church plant.

Mike was in one vehicle with a few team members going one direction, while Mikey, our son, and I were in a different vehicle headed in yet a different compass indication with the rest of our group of intrepid soul-seeking warriors. This is a common practice when there is a lot of territory to cover, and we have capable team members that can be separated into different ministry groups.

All the while, dust was swirling in the air from our tires rolling over the powder dry dirt paths, making breathing difficult because of the cloud of brown haze boiling into the open windows and the inevitable cracks that appear in older vehicles. At the end of most days, my skin gives the false impression of having acquired a real African tan, until I take a sponge bath in the evening before retiring to bed, only to discover that my exotic sub-Saharan glow was only dirt, and beneath the dirt still lay my normal white freckled skin, maybe just a little more sunburned.

As we continued on the arduous journey, we jostled along over rocks and potholes so big that one would feel that some of them could swallow the vehicle. At the same time the chatter in the van would remind one of a flock of magpies trying to outdo one another during mating season. Occasionally, although we could not always see it, we caught the distinct odor of a nearby village consisting of the scent of various animals, smoke, and some things at which one could only guess, but might not wish to know. Most villages are not located near a road, but rather deep into the bush and out of sight of the passersby unless you are with those of us who are actively seeking them out, which was exactly what our mission was on this notable day.

Traveling in the rough country of Kenya in exploration is never a boring enterprise. We find ourselves constantly on the edge of a spectacle. Whether we are meritorious of the attention we receive by our western antics in the bush country of east Africa (such a complete cultural difference to our own), or we are merely the most interesting novelty the natives have seen that day, we get A LOT of attention. One aspect of that is the way that children will run out of sheer terror as we enter into these unreached area villages. The precious kids will peer out from their locales with big eyes and looks of awe as they see for the first time in most cases an African safari vehicle. It is always the same: they see us and run straight for their little mud houses, or run to hide behind the clothing of their fathers or mothers, and peer out from beside their legs as if it is the safest place on earth.

As we rounded a bend in the path, we noticed something under a lone acacia tree. Not sure what to make of what we saw, we slowed our pace. The sun was high and hot overhead as we pulled closer.

"It's a child," Mikey said.

So when we pulled up, and this child lying under the tree did not move, I thought, *Surely he is dead,* and Mikey told the team, "Get ready to pray for a resurrection."

As we approached the child, we noted that he remained unmoving. This is a very unlikely response, especially in these remote areas, because most of the children have never seen a vehicle such as this before.

We got out ready to pray a most desperate prayer. Just then, the young boy stirred. Our hearts were relieved to know the child was alive.

The ruckus of our arrival was noted, and the villagers began to gather around. We felt it was appropriate to carry out our service and presentation of the gospel even before we prayed for this obviously ailing child. We shared the story of Jesus and man's need for Him. To our sheer delight, the whole gathering saw the wisdom of the truth, and accepted the Lord as Savior.

As a point, this is often the case when going into unreached areas, as people are untainted and seem to hear the truth and receive it more readily.

After leading folks to pray for salvation, the time came to pray for the sick. We discovered the boy was extremely ill and had been removed from his village so as not to infect the rest. This is the Maasai health care system: those who are a danger are cast out to die and hopefully not infect the others living in the village.

This boy had traveled over three days to this spot because he heard, "God was coming to the tree." He had heard this because, as we press deeper into the unknown areas, we meet shepherds and travelers on foot with whom we share our destinations. They then pass along the message to further reaches, and so many hear we are coming well before we reach them. At this statement, our hearts were so humbled at the joy of being emissaries for the King of kings. God was coming to the tree—through His servants. Our team laid hands on the boy, and immediately he recovered to full strength, his fever broke, and he rose up from the ground. It was then he thanked us, rolled up his blanket which he had lain upon, and began his journey home.

This way of dealing with death seems foreign to us; however, it is customary for the Maasai to leave the weak, dying, and dead out for the *Crocuta*, the scientific name for hyena—AKA *Ondilili* or *Oln'gojine* in the Maasai language—to feast upon once a blanket of darkness conceals their presence. Truly an opportunistic feeder, hyenas readily scavenge for human corpses, and are even known to dig up a shallow grave and eat the remains. However, one must never underestimate them, for they are talented killers and not just grave robbers, as many sleeping Africans have discovered. A corpse rejected by scavengers is seen as having something wrong with it, and liable to cause social disgrace; therefore, it is not uncommon for bodies to be covered in fat and blood from a slaughtered goat. Burial has in the past been reserved for great chiefs, since it is believed to be harmful to the soil. This traditional practice of leaving the dead out for scavengers is unfathomable for the western mindset. Nevertheless, it is part and parcel of tribal practices to this very day unless you are a Christian, and even then in the deep bush, I'm sure they still practice this tradition. This is one of the reasons we must reach the Maasai with the hope of the gospel. They are so terrified of death they will often move a whole village to another location rather than deal with a dead body. They need to know that as a believer, we sorrow not as others who have no hope, but one day the dead will be raised to eternal life; and so shall we ever be with the Lord.

The moment of this dying child's miracle stood out as a present day reminder of the man at the pool of Bethesda, and Jesus having mercy on him. These moments are some of the beautiful things that anchor my faith so strongly into the truth of Jesus' love and the cause of our mission for His kingdom. It would be enough for this story to conclude with a boy given over to die being restored by the mighty hand of God, but the story does not stop here.

It was a day or so later that our team had passed into still further reaches than where the boy had been healed. We pulled into another village, and received perhaps the most incredible welcome I have ever experienced. As we exited the vehicle upon stopping near an acacia tree, we asked folks to gather for a service. In an unprecedented experience, they declined us, but rather said the chief's wife wanted us to come for an audience.

We arrived at the village center, and were instructed to have a seat and wait. This was a most unusual request; and, honestly, I wasn't sure what was actually happening. These adventures in service of our sovereign God often lead us into the unknown; and we simply learn to trust and flow with the machinations of the Master for His purposes.

About this time, cups of fresh tea began to be placed in our hands. One after another, every team member was given a plastic cup of steaming hot chai. Refusing to receive the gift would have been a slap in the face culturally, and so we drank the warm offering with joy. The tea was positively delightful. Mikey said it best: "It was like warm honey crossing the completely thrilled tastebuds crammed together on my tongue." Each team member proclaimed his pleasant surprise at the perfectly sweet taste from each sip of chai.

After all had been served, a young woman stepped out of the house and looked to each of us. There were tears in her eyes. I must admit I was entranced at the sum of this experience. An interpreter began to share what she wished to say to us.

She thanked us for the life of her son. We learned it was her boy who had lain under the tree as if dead a few days before. She said her child had been fully welcomed back into the village after God had healed him. She said her whole village wanted to be saved like the other village had been. We prayed with her and her people.

Then we asked, "Why are you crying?" She said she was embarrassed that she had no sugar for her tea in order to honor us. We all looked at each other as we recalled the sweetened nectar which we had just enjoyed, and I began to laugh. I shared with her that she had no cause to be embarrassed, as God had sweetened each cup perfectly for each person. Her offering had been blessed by God!

We saw the boy before we left, and I was left in wonder. God has this remarkable plan, which none but Himself can guess, and it ends in completing His intentions.

As I write about this, I am reminded of the story of our first Maasai convert in the Maasai Mara area.

His name was Peter Liaram (pronounced *lee ar am*), and he was a truly unique individual. In the first place, he was six foot, ten inches tall. On top of that, he probably weighed no more than 140 or 150 pounds. He was a man with a beautiful spirit, and he loved to hug. When he did so, because of his height and weight it was like being hugged by a giant praying mantis. You just had to pray he never had the same sort of intent as the predatory insect; he certainly never revealed any such tendencies. He was just a giant lover of Jesus after his salvation.

When we returned to his area about six months later, we wondered how we would find him faring. We needn't have worried as when we first encountered him again, he said to Mike and me in his broken English colored by his Maasai accent, "I would like to show you my choir." He then proceeded to parade out of some *bomas* (Maasai *manyattas* or houses) about ten to fifteen little kids probably four to ten years old and maybe three to four feet tall, which made quite a contrast when they surrounded their very tall mentor and *choir director*. They reminded one of a pitcher surrounded by some very short glasses. Anyway, they blessed us with some absolutely beautiful and totally wonderful off-key songs in the inimitable Maasai way, exalting the Savior of the world. Peter had won all these children to the love of the Jesus he had come to know.

Peter established a church in the Talek area of the Mara, right on the border of the famed Maasai Mara Game Reserve, which grew very rapidly to around 200—mostly very young converts. In cooperation with the mission, we provided Peter with a very fine stone church for which we supplied most of the funds.

To show you the kind of man Peter was, because he had never been to Bible school, he asked a friend of his to come and help him pastor the church while he walked five miles every day to establish a church in a town called Aitong because there was no witness there. I might add there are two excellent congregations there from those early beginnings.

You are probably asking yourself at this point, "What does that have to do with the beginning of this story about the boy under the tree?" I ask for your continued indulgence for a moment longer.

I shall never forget the day Mike and I were at the Utalii Hotel in Nairobi, when our friend, Missionary J. R. Gould, informed us Peter and his friend, William, had been caught in a rainstorm. As they ran for shelter, Peter began to have difficulty breathing. They changed the course of their flight to the nearby one-room clinic where Peter collapsed and died before anyone could do anything. He was only thirty-three years old!

Remember that all of this is happening in the deep bush of Africa; and keep in mind the attitudes of the Maasai toward death, and their customs regarding a body.

Because Peter was the first Christian among the Maasai in the area, William, our friend and another of our Maasai "sons" who had come to work with Peter and with the church, went to the family and begged for Peter's body. He told them that Peter was a man of God, and should have a Christian burial, and not be given to the hyena. The family finally relented. Since there is little or no equipment to deal with this situation, William flagged a *matatu* (a taxi van); although it was crowded with many other passengers, he set Peter's body up in the seat, and sat beside him for almost five hours to get him to a morgue. That is true Christian love, especially with his Maasai background.

While Peter's body was being prepared and his coffin being made, Mike told William to tell the family to dig the grave deep so the hyena could not dig it up. When the day came for the first Christian funeral in that area, Mike walked over to check the grave the family had dug. He was *shangad* (pronounced *"shongod,"* meaning "totally shocked") when he saw the ten-foot deep grave. When he asked why it was so deep, they said, "Well, you said you didn't want the hyenas to get him."

The funeral was so sad but glorious at the same time. A grain of wheat, Jesus spoke of in parable, had died. But as Jesus had shown me the day we got the news of Peter's death, it had truly produced a harvest, as many of Peter's friends and family came to the saving knowledge of Jesus Christ at the end of the service. Even today, many years later, this event is still producing fruit.

Peter had been working in the area where the young man under the tree in the original story lived. After Mikey laid hands on this little boy, and he was healed—as we told you earlier—the team took him to the village. It turned out the chief of this village had five wives and many children. All of them, the whole village, became blood-bought children of the living God.

Isn't it amazing how God can do two miracles, take one of His children to heaven and heal another on earth, but achieve the same results? I can guarantee you, Liaram is in the grandstand spoken of in Hebrews. I also guarantee you: HE IS SMILING!!!

7

A NOTE FROM THE AUTHOR

Looking back on the many trials our family has walked through, more times than I can count, I have had to reach down to the bedrock of who I am in Jesus Christ to survive. I can clearly see how we are made stronger and better from the trials and sufferings; not weaker as one would imagine. The scripture says that in our weaknesses His strength is made perfect. Our much buffeting will either make us bitter or better. We can choose to throw ourselves on the mercies of God, and allow Him to put steel in our souls, making our spiritual chain link strong to withstand the pulls of life. God allows trials and tribulations in our lives to do just that—make us strong. No Olympic weightlifter ever started out a winner. He works, trains, and pushes his muscles to the limit until he finally wins the prize. God, knowing us better than we know ourselves, allows trials from time to time to build our spiritual muscles so we can, in Him, win the prize.

If we could ever learn to not ask God "why" this or that has happened, but to say, "God, help me be more like You because this or that has happened." When we get to heaven, we will know the "why," but then, I feel sure it won't matter.

What I know is: God loves us, and, keeping eternity in mind, will allow only that which is ultimately for our good, never allowing us to be tested above that which we are able to stand. I'm not speaking about temptation. This is a completely different category. I'm speaking of *testings* we have little or no control over. This is where the issue of trust comes in, which is the goal of God for each of us to trust Him completely, fearlessly, joyfully, without doubting or wavering, as a child would trust a kind father.

For us to walk in complete obedience and complete trust is vital. Trust that God knows every weak link in our chain, and must reinforce it with His power, making us completely dependent on Him for our strength. He knows that in ourselves we will not be able to stand in that evil day, but in Him—His perfect strength—and only in Him can we triumph and win the prize. Our all-seeing, all-knowing, infinite God is not willing that any should lose or perish, but that all would triumph or come to repentance. He will strengthen our weak areas until that day in which He calls us home. He sees the whole picture, not just a part. Not just today, but eternity.

So why do we fear the trials of life, knowing that our present suffering is not worthy to be compared with the glory that shall be revealed? This is why He says to rejoice. One might be able to say we spend a lifetime preparing to die. This truth is yet another area which separates us from the world and the carnal mind. We, as God's children, the apple of His eye whose names are not just written in the Book of Life but carved in His great hand, don't suffer like those who have no hope. It is the hope factor that our faith hinges on. We can rejoice knowing that each spiritual washout or trying of our faith makes us stronger, and that a little more of the carnal man, the flesh man, the weak link, is destroyed. We can rejoice knowing God is working on us, making us strong in Him, and perfecting us for the coming day.

Trust, faith, and joyful dependence in God are the goals of His devoted followers. Before the trying of my faith, I preached theory: someone else's story of deliverance. Since the trying of my faith, I now preach the "I Know" gospel—joy unspeakable and full of glory, a peace that passes human understanding, the Comforter has come. For when I fell at His feet brokenhearted, stripped of myself, having no answer as to the question why or what to do, He simply gave me what I, in myself, did not possess—a joy unspeakable and full of glory, a peace that passes human understanding, and set the Comforter to come and comfort me with a comfort that doesn't come from a bottle or a pill. No longer do I preach theory, but to me, it is fact.

To believe is easier; to trust is sweet. I felt Him take my burden and heart-wrenching sorrows too heavy for me to bear, and give to me freedom. I drank from His cup of joy; not my own, but made mine through Him. I know that I know He causes all things to work for my good in light of eternity, and gives to me the grace to endure. What a God who loves me so much that He never takes His eyes off of me. We are the apple of His eye; the object of His affection. He is a loving God that will help me to grow to godly adulthood, preparing me for heaven.

I thank Him that He will not sit idly by while I, as a child, play in the middle of the street where I could be crushed, forever separated from His loving arms; but He will fight for me and correct me as any good, caring parent would do. He longs to hold me in His loving protective arms for all eternity. My heart cries for all His creation who don't know His love; for His children who don't understand that He is continually working on us to make us strong so that when we face that evil day of temptation, we will not be broken. Each link must in Him be strong. Not one link can be made of our flesh or our strength, for we are not able to withstand the forces of evil. Praise God that He works to reinforce our chain links even when we fuss and complain to Him about it. Our eyes have not yet seen the whole truth. One day we will be filled with exceeding joy when we finally see the whole picture. Our hearts should bow in humble submission to a loving, caring Father, accepting the trial of each day as preparation for a greater day coming. The ultimate prize awaits those who by faith do just that.

8

SOME THROUGH THE FIRE

MARIGOLD'S INTRODUCTION

"Because He Lives."The words slipped lovingly
from my lips as I sang for Baby Mikey's
dedication. It was March 1975, as with the
deepest conviction I intoned the Spirit-inspired
words of the marvelous anthem penned by the
Gaithers: *"Because He Lives I Can Face
Tomorrow."* It is merciful that the tomorrows are a
mystery unfolding like the layers of an onion, one
peel at a time. God did promise He would never
leave us nor forsake us, and we would never be
tempted above which we are able to bear.
Although I have to admit, there were times during
the happenings in the years shortly hereafter that
I felt He had much more confidence in me than I
did. Had it not been for the vast unfathomable
riches of the storehouse of the Lord's loving
mercies, we surely could not have survived the
gut-wrenching tragedy that lay ahead for our
precious son and us.

All of us have obtained great solace in times of
trial in our lives from the monumental words of
the great prophet Isaiah found in the 43rd
chapter, verse 2 (NKJV) of his towering God-
inspired book which states: *"When you pass*

through the waters, they will not overflow you, when you pass through the fire, you will not be burned." Now you Bible scholars know that is not the whole verse, but you get the drift. Even though we know these words were written to comfort Israel, we can still receive encouragement from them. However, when the words cease to be metaphor and become all too real, then what? That is what this all too true story is about.

While holding snugly in my arms my darling, newborn baby boy dressed in the dedication gown made of purest white cotton and lace flowing halfway to the floor fashioned by one of my dearest friends, Dorothy Bonnett, I softly began the tender words of the first verse of this powerful song that we had chosen for this special occasion:

> *How sweet to hold a newborn baby, and*
> *feel the love and joy he brings.*
> *But greater still that calm assurance: [our*
> *son] can face uncertain days*
> *Because He lives.*

Looking into his beautiful little face with his ocean blue eyes staring back at me, my voice began to rise in volume as I started the powerfully, truthful assuring chorus:

Because He lives, I can face tomorrow
[and] because He lives, all fear is gone.
Because I know, [I know] He holds the
future
[My child can face uncertain days
because Christ lives].[1]

First a beautiful auburn-hair daughter, and now a blond-headed, blue-eyed son; what more could a young family ask for? We were blessed, truly blessed.

We were pastoring a great church in Bastrop, Louisiana—a paper mill community nestled in the delta belt of north Louisiana; a place with friendly population of about 10,000, where folks still make a deal on a hardy handshake; where people still wave and say, "How are you doing?"; a community with hunting, fishing, and outdoor living woven into the very fabric of life.

The church had an attendance of 250 or so when we became pastors. The auditorium only seated around 600. God sovereignly sent revival to our church. For example, teens from the community went to their youth meetings, climbed out of their church's bathroom window, and came to our church hungry to be baptized in the Holy Spirit. On any given Sunday, about 200 youth ages thirteen to nineteen attended. With the building no longer able to hold the crowds of people coming, for a time we rented the high school auditorium to accommodate the over 900 that now called Bastrop First their home church.

We as a church began growing even faster than First Unnamed Church in our small southern town, so the pastor started fighting "those crazy holy rollers" from his pulpit!!! Then, because of piqued curiosity, his daughter with some of her friends came to one of our revivals and was herself baptized in the Holy Spirit. Now, of course, we were not there, but we heard that the following Sunday her father with great chagrin threw up his hands and said, "All I can say is, it's in the Bible!!"

The principal of the high school told us, "I don't really know what's going on over at your church, but keep it up because the atmosphere in my school has changed!!!"

Mikey, our son, was born during this awesome move of God. We dedicated him to the Lord a week after he entered this world.

We knew that the church needed to relocate, but just could not bring ourselves to do so as my mother and dad had poured twenty-six years of their lives into the work at Bastrop, and I had played in the trenches of the foundation as a preschooler. My dad had built the beautiful southern colonial-style church with large white pillars across the front; ceiling-to-floor stained glass windows on either side completed the massive structure.

A few years later, we resigned the pastorate in Bastrop and accepted the call to pastor a new church plant in Covington, Louisiana located across the causeway from New Orleans. The church was in real Cajun country—we're talking swamps, lazy rivers, Spanish moss draped old oak trees, crawfish étouffée, jambalaya, and beignets. We saw the entire area as a mission field—our hearts always drawn to the lost. God placed within us a love for the folks that called south Louisiana home.

Fortunately, we could not see seven years into the future from Mikey's dedication to know the severe trauma that would try our family's faith like nothing we had ever faced. Crushing pain beyond our imagination and the ability to understand would be our lot in life for much longer than we could ever have imagined in our worst nightmares. Praise God we only live one day at a time—moment by moment—rising up to meet life's challenges. We cannot see what lies ahead of us from sunrise to sunrise.

I share this story that God might be glorified.

MIKEY'S INTRODUCTION

The very moment of combustion is so incredibly vivid in my mind. I have tried to write this story so many times only to get to certain parts and relent because of smelling burned flesh, feeling the searing bite of the flame, or hearing the screams that belonged to me and/or others who suffered near me in the hospital. This has created a unique barrier to full revelation of the events that transpired. In order to put healing and the time required for it to manifest in perspective, it was only a few short years ago that I stopped being consistently embarrassed by my disfigurement.

This story is not one so tender as to be enjoyed, but rather one to be softened in order to be bearable to the hearer. At this time, however, I believe the intent is to communicate the event—to disclose the very intimate sufferings. There was not anyone attached to me that went unaffected by this painful and shattering moment. The church, so happy and calm when the pastor thrives, was required to have its faith tested by witnessing their pastor and family suffer under the weight of the world's curse. People, however misguided in doctrines, had to contemplate the truth of trial for all who lived under the fall of man.

MARIGOLD'S WORDS

The stinging cold with its frigid icy fingers clawed at our body parts as though Jack Frost had some kind of vendetta to settle with the choir. I felt for sure our vocal cords would freeze open from the arctic-like conditions in which we performed.

South Louisiana in December can be miserably cold, almost unbearable, due to the high humidity for which that area of the country is so well known. It was a bit like walking into a walk-in freezer at a meat locker with the door open on a rainy day. It was a damp and bitter cold sort of night. Temperatures were in the low twenties—now granted, that doesn't sound cold in more mountainous areas such as the higher elevations of say, Colorado, but in an area with the humidity feeling more than 1,000 percent . . . it's brutal! I've been in sub-zero weather in drier climates that was easier to endure than a thermometer reading of twenty degrees on a wet Louisiana night. Some of the Cajun choir members thought we had been transplanted to the North Pole for this Christmas cantata. You could almost hear the bells jingling from the reindeer pulling a sleigh across the cold gray sky—or would that be, as I have seen on a few billboards while traveling in south Louisiana, alligators pulling a pirogue (a flat-bottom shallow, drafting canoe propelled by a man with a poll pushing the boat through the swamp). The billboard, of course, had the gators and pirogue flying through the air with old Saint Nick cracking his whip across the backs of the refugees from prehistoric earth "gators" darting across the sky like the proverbial team from the North Pole.

Christmas is such a wonderful time of year, bringing the usual rounds of local festivities and celebrations. The church family we pastored was called Northlake Assembly of God in Covington, Louisiana. Due to the oceans of mercy and blessings from our Lord, the congregation had grown substantially in attendance since our arrival some three years before. We devised a plan for a community outreach—A Living Christmas Tree—erected on the K-Mart parking lot. A great group of men whose trade was carpentry built the tree of wood and scaffolding—a combination of steel and wood large enough to accommodate the entire church choir. It began with a tier of singers each holding a light on the bottom platform; then each tier rising above the last by several steps with decreasing numbers of singers on each ascending tier, until only one sat at the apex giving the illusion of a very large Christmas tree.

The time had come—December 21—our chosen date for the vocal presentation. There was much excitement as weeks of labor had gone into the preparations for this event.

Little did we know that in less than fourteen hours a tragedy would occur which would affect our family forever. Our seven-year-old Mikey's life would hang by a thread, and his world and ours would be permanently altered. Had it not been for the ocean of the Lord's tender loving mercies, I surely could not have survived the days that lay ahead.

Even as I write the story, I have to pause and ask myself, "How did we as a family survive?" And the answer is always the same: Jesus . . . God . . . Because He lives.

Even though this new church plant had grown from about thirty attendees to four or five hundred, and eight hundred on special days, we still prayed continually for more souls to be added to the body of Christ—lives to lay at the Master's feet. We tried to reach our community with the gospel message of Jesus Christ as a personal Savior with the aforementioned visual outreach in the form of Christmas music glorifying Jesus. Our prayer was that many would be reached with the good news that Jesus saves. People who ordinarily would not see a sober day through the holiday season could hear the gospel, and their lives forever changed. That was the goal—the reason—the drive behind the work . . . the people . . . the heartbeat of God.

At dusk, we gathered waiting for dark and a more appropriate ambiance. A little later with the faint smell of pine in the air, we began. With each rising note, the temperature plunged a little lower. Very few people stopped, and those who did, remained in their warm cars, leaving us to brave the elements. As I directed the choir in the freezing cold, I mentally debated with myself if our work of preparing, rehearsing, and performing this Christmas cantata had been worth the effort. I thought, *Why, tonight of all nights, has this freakish "deep freeze" for our area taken us prisoner with its chilled-to-the-bone claws digging deep as if to put a halt to the evening's success? Was this to be the "Grinch" that threatened to steal our Christmas efforts?* I silently prayed, *Lord, I know You want this community reached with the Word more than we do. Please lift this biting cold weather.*

We continued to sing while holding our lit candles so the world could see we were giving homage to the King of the season. In spite of everything, I must say that it was beautiful.

Continuing to direct the choir with frozen, trembling hands, I could hardly snatch a breath because it was so cold. Dancing ice crystals in the little pockets of my lungs were putting on a show of their own while trying to produce enough air to accommodate the demand to sing. At least I could build some body heat by moving my arms to direct. The choir could only stand still and sing. How were we thin-blooded, south Louisianans standing still to sing! It was amazing, and I was truly in awe.

Perseverance and grit finally surrendered to reason.

"Okay, guys," I reluctantly told the choir members' families, "you who are not singing are welcome to go to our home and get warm. Everyone's welcome, except the choir." Because of course, they had to sing. "We always keep lots of Mike's favorite popcorn on hand, as well as coffee, so make yourselves at home: the house is unlocked." The truth was we never locked the house except when sleeping at night. We hadn't had a key in three years. Sometimes we came home from a hard day's work to find a church member sitting on the couch waiting for us to arrive just to visit a while or pray with them.

They wasted no time gathering non-singing family members—including our son, Mikey—and heading to our home. It wasn't long until the entire house was permeated with the buttery aroma of popcorn leaving the longsuffering choir—us—a distant memory as they indulged their appetites. Fresh brewed New Orleans chicory coffee with its hot, strong aroma wafted into the room as if rivaling for the best scents on the cold night.

However . . .

Mr. Frosty visiting from Siberia had a little more torture up his cold-hearted sleeve for the choir members. The brave and faithful choir members themselves had a story of more shivering and shaking yet to go on while we overcame the elements to share the Word of God.

"O Come, All Ye Faithful" moved on to "Glory to God in the Highest" as we continued to sing the cantata, a production arranged from traditional Christmas hymns. Through the intense cold, we declared the glory and deity of our dear Lord and Savior Jesus Christ with our feet feeling as if encased in ice.

While the choir sang, the members' families warmed themselves at our home, and the boys brewed mischief.

It didn't take long for the barely pubescent teenage boys to tire of the indoors. Hot chocolate and fresh popped corn had revved their engines, and they were ready for a little outdoor creative entertainment while dads and the younger children continued fellowshipping and warming up inside our home. Mikey, our seven-year-old son, not wanting to miss a thing, closely followed the young teens.

Now, I've heard the phrase "Boys will be boys" many times in my life. It is usually used to excuse the mischief into which young boys get themselves. Have you emptied a little boy's pocket and found frogs, or worse yet, worms? What did you do? With a light chuckle, you probably said, "Oh well, boys will be boys."

When my mother was living, she loved to relate the story of a young pioneer pastor's mischievous son whom I will call Jimmy to protect the innocent. Jimmy was one of those kids that evoked people to raise their eyebrows in disapproval of his ADHD flurry of activity. The absolute mayhem, which in fact he could cause, always gave my mom a hearty chuckle. One Sunday afternoon with guests on the premises waiting on the promise of lunch, Jimmy played around in the old outhouse, lost his footing, and fell through the hole of the home-crafted wooden toilet seat and into the sludge which, after rescuing him, caused the guests to roar with laughter! "Oh well, boys will be boys."

Young Mikey, along with his teenaged partners in crime, concocted their own kind of mischief. Mikey was all boy and constantly into something. But on this night, what Mikey and his friends got into—although boyish play—was certainly no laughing matter. Pilfering through my kitchen cabinets, the youngsters found a stainless steel mixing bowl. Then proceeding outside into the blistering-cold weather, they filled the shiny round bowl with lawn mower gasoline which was kept in a can on top of an upright freezer.

Without the adults' knowledge, the boys lit the gas and popped their firecrackers by throwing them into the fire blazing up from the stainless steel bowl. Just as quietly as the boys had slipped out of the house, they slipped back in unnoticed by anyone. Only the boys were aware of the evidentiary mess left hidden by the darkness in the backyard, and unlikely to be soon discovered due to the numbing cold night.

Our shivering bodies blue from the frigid weather, the choir wrapped up the grand finale. The Living Christmas Tree production was completed. Over. A sigh slipped from my mouth as I exhaled and said, "Praise God!" The idea seemed so important the previous September when we sat around the drawing board, making plans to lift up the name of Jesus so that all of Lake Ponchartrain's North Shore would see and join in the celebration of Christ's glorious birth. However, as we left the empty parking lot, I thought the only one who really heard or saw us was our beloved Lord Jesus. Well, after all, were we not singing our praises for Him? We did our best and we had a sense of accomplishment—a feeling of satisfaction that we had completed a difficult task.

The party back at the house ended as we arrived home. Families dispersed eager to travel their separate ways on this unnaturally bitterly cold night, just as I dreamed of the comforts of home.

After waving goodbye to the last of our houseguests, I scurried inside to finally sink beneath the exquisite warmth of swirling bath waters. It was late, and exhaustion crept into my aching body. I soaked in the soothing, hot tub of water, trying to thaw my nearly frozen extremities. The family went to bed leaving me alone with the thoughts of the evening's events rolling over and over in my mind like a movie rerun playing again and again.

There would not be mental rest this night, as I still felt wired. With church obligations completed, I refocused my mind on the final touches for our family holiday. This was my year to host the celebration. Everyone was coming to our house. Slowly my thinking began to travel a different route, leaving the night behind, and gearing up for a wonderful family Christmas. There was a lot of preparation with a short time to accomplish it.

Our family group is small, but very close. There was my mother and father, Juanita and James Allen; my sister and her husband, Marcia and Maurice Lednicky; Mike, me, and our two children, Mikey and Melissa. The Lednickys' only child, Michelle, had gone to be with the Lord when she was ten years of age—a victim of leukemia—leaving a hole in our family gatherings.

Other years, the Lednickys or Mom and Dad took their turns hosting Christmas. I was always excited when my year rolled around. I preferred Christmas in my home, and still do. It was a delight and a sheer joy to provide the venue for our family celebration. I love to entertain, and I especially love to entertain my precious loved ones.

On December 22, my eyes popped open early in spite of the lack of sleep the night before. So much cleaning, baking, cooking, and decorating were yet to be done. Tomorrow everyone would come. I needed to bake pies, cookies, cakes, ham, turkey, dressing, and prepare the veggies.

While Mom lived, she traditionally made her matchless chicken and dumplings. Nowadays my sister Marcia does a superb job making them even though I can. I prefer making the chicken and dressing.

"Knock, knock!! Marigold," Jean said as she entered the house. Jean Rogers is the kind of friend that jumps in to lend a helping hand with whatever is going on. I perked some coffee for us. Chatting and laughing together, she soon was helping me with preparations for my soon-to-arrive family.

Melissa and her friend, Greta, decided to go bicycle riding. They only had Melissa's bright red bike, but it didn't take long for them to decide it was perfectly okay to borrow Mikey's boy style blue bike. The two girls headed out for a day of bicycle riding and fun, unaware that upon returning home Melissa's world would be turned upside down for many years to come.

Mike was at the church wrapping up his office work, hoping to be free to relax with the rest of us when the family arrived.

I was making my favorite dessert, a delightful old Cheshier family recipe called chocolate chip pie—a confection loaded with chips, coconut, and pecans (delightfully delicious) causing one to gain weight just smelling it. I remember standing in Marjorie's kitchen, Mike's mom, when she pulled the first pecan chocolate chip pie out of the oven. Wow, it tasted like a little piece of heaven.

Boredom stirred within our young son. Everyone was busy but him. Having nothing to do can be scary for a seven-year-old boy with a world of energy and a mountain of imagination. Wandering out into the backyard, he suddenly remembered the leftover firecrackers from the previous evening. He found only five remaining. *I'll pop these firecrackers; that will be a lot of fun!* he thought.

He crashed through the back doors with a new burst of energy. "Mom, Mom. Last night we popped firecrackers in the backyard, and I found five that didn't pop. Can I pop them, please?"

"No," I retorted.

"Please, Mother," Mikey pleaded.

"Mikey, we don't have any matches, so do something else."

Mikey started the mad search for matches with determination. Our house was all-electric, and we were "no-how, no-way" smokers. Finding matches in our house was *mission impossible*. He rifled through every drawer, hunting diligently. He even pilfered through my purses where he hit the jackpot. He came into the kitchen proudly displaying the one match, which he'd found in my purse in a box advertising the restaurant from whence it came.

"I found one! Now, can I finish popping my firecrackers?"

How I wish firecrackers would be banned! When I was a small child, about five years old, I held onto a firecracker too long, and it blew up in my hand. The pain was terrible. Here was my small son begging, pleading to play with them.

These were only junior firecrackers, nothing like the big ones I had as a girl. I saw no way they could do any real harm. How many times have I wished I had said, "Emphatically, NO!" . . . But I didn't. Instead, I gave in. He had looked so hard to find a match; how could I disappoint him? I said, "Well, Mikey, make that one match do. It's the only one we've got."

I figured that one match meant one firecracker, but that's not how Mikey read the situation.

MIKEY'S WORDS

As I said, I remember the combustive moment with vivid detail. I was playing in the back yard.

The season was for fireworks, and it was a time when children generally were more trustworthy. So there I was: a seven-year-old, playing with black cat firecrackers. These had the paper wick and were incredibly unpredictable. One may take two seconds to explode while others may give almost instant concussive payoff. As I enjoyed the festive items, I ran out of matches. Still having several little bombs left, I decided to see if I could find more. I had already sacked the normal places in our house for acquiring matches. A few moments later, I returned to the back porch to resume the festivities as I had found one more book of matches in Mom's purse. Upon inspection, I realized there was but one more match inside.

I needed yet more fire. Looking around, my eyes spotted the upright freezer with the gas can my dad kept for our lawn mower on top.

Now I was raised with all the typical warnings of playing with fire. However, this seemed a special occasion, and merited disobedience. Besides, the night before some teens from the church had come to a party at our house, and showed me how to safely play with the flammable contents. Of course, the difference was quantity—where as they had used but a quarter cup of fuel for an effect, as a child operating in excess, I poured the entire gallon into a stainless steel mixing bowl. I placed the bowl at the base of an outdoor water faucet. Though I had veered from wise choice, I was not without context for what could happen. The night before, the small blaze was easily extinguished. I was sure this exercise would end no differently.

In my mind, the whole thing slows down. The tear of the base of the paper match. . . . The scratch of its tip against the sand-board. . . . The flair of the flame. . . . The rush of sulfuric odor. . . . A moment to see it truly lit. . . . The muscles in my arm moving my hand toward the clear, unassuming liquid in the bowl. . . . My gaze shifting from the match to where it would land. My heart beat increasing with the thrill of expectation. . . . All at once a bassy "whoosh" greeting my ears and the bright light of ignition. . . . A smile of a satisfied success. . . . My other hand moving to the bowl with the remaining fireworks. . . . The fire growing! . . . The release of the fireworks and the faithful landing into the flame. . . . Then nothing! No explosion! No pop! And no turning back!

In this moment, the fire comes into view! . . . Growing! . . . Hungry! . . . My heart racing all the more! . . . Fear rising! . . . My hand reaching for the water faucet! . . . The heat from the blaze becomes uncomfortable! . . . The turn of the handle!

A rush of water burst from the faucet. . . . Hope!
. . . A flash! . . . And wash of fire and heat! . . .
Terror.

At this moment, I was in panic mode, but I had
not yet lost my wits. I knew water would not
extinguish the fire. My mind raced for answers,
answers that would not alert my parents to a
really bad decision! . . . A blanket—I remembered
seeing a TV program where a person had beaten
the fire from someone else with a blanket. I
abandoned the flames for just a moment, ran into
the house and then to the laundry room. No
blanket was there! I needed something, and there
was a broom. I left through the laundry room door
next to the corner of the house where this drama
was playing out.

Looking upon the fire, I was in awe: So bright! So
hot! So hungry—like some beast made of writhing
living flame! I raised the broom above my head! I
would vanquish this beast! Bringing the broom
down with force, I struck the bowl's side nearest
me. In an instant, the bowl catapulted towards
me. I saw the light! I felt the heat! I knew the bite
was coming! I gasped in the sheer horror of that
moment.

This is the moment—the one moment—where the
world stopped spinning, and innocence died for
me. This was the moment that shaped all of my

future—inescapable, undeniable, at times unbearable—this is the moment I burned.

The whoosh of the flame was like a roar of some beast as it charged its overmatched victim. There was no time to shield my face. My arms, like that of a statue, held a pose chiseled in place and unmovable. Bringing down the broom to strike the bowl left my person open to the full fury of this aggressor.

As the liquid flame splashed on me, there was a paradox of cold and hot—the liquid surprisingly cool was immediately followed by heat and pain. I watched it come. I saw the light of day go from blue-white to orange.

I was scared and I was in flight mode. It never crossed my mind to stop, drop, and roll—I ran and I hoped. I remember the thoughts in my child-mind—I remember the words that came. *I'm in trouble*, I thought, *I need an adult to help me . . . Maybe they will see me if I run near their yard.* I ran in a wide arc in my back yard hoping someone in the houses next door and behind would see me. I ran where I knew to run, not because I could see very well. . . . Flames were in my eyes . . . I looked through fire. As far as I could tell, the whole world was engulfed in flames. I made a turn towards my house. I knew my mom was in the kitchen, and I knew she would help me. I got to the back door—still on fire. I opened the door—still burning. I hurried to the kitchen and yelled—the flesh and meat cooking under the intense heat.

My mom came to my rescue! She had my fire out in a moment!

MARIGOLD

My little son went to the back patio and climbed on a small motorcycle to reach the gasoline on top of the upright freezer. Copying the older boys from the night before, he poured some gasoline into the stainless steel mixing bowl that had been out in the corner of the back yard all night. Unnoticed by anyone, Mikey put his firecrackers in the bowl of gasoline, struck the match, and dropped it into the bowl. Nothing happened. The wicks had only gotten wet. This was nothing like last night's blast when the firecrackers hit the fire.

What have I done wrong? he queried.

*What if the fire goes out? I have no more matches,*he said to himself.

He picked up the gas can and slowly added more of the volatile liquid to the fire.

Horror of horrors! The fire leaped up. The liquid engulfed the can like lightning, and caught the grass on fire.

We believe that Mikey was entrapped by the intensity of the inferno at that point. Our precious little one picked up a broom and tried to beat the grass fire out before it caught the house on fire. Instead of smothering the danger, in his young fright he accidentally hit the bowl of blazing petroleum, sending a resulting fireball onto his face and upper body as though shot from a rocket launcher. To this day, he still says he saw the face of evil in that furnace blast as it cascaded into his face.

Mikey was a beautiful boy—short to the ground and slightly chubby like a cherub in a Michelangelo painting in the Sistine Chapel. As a baby, he had cotton-white hair; but by seven years old, it was a slightly darker dishwater blond, and quite thick. His eyes were still deep-ocean blue and tender. Mikey was a child who lived to please. He wanted desperately to please us, his parents. He was quick to obey, never deliberately disobeying. I thought when he was a baby that he was too pretty to be a boy; Michael, his father, saw him as "all boy." I can see him now, standing in front of his great-grandmother and great-aunt

Opal—for whom I am named—his blue eyes sparkling and blond hair shining. He tapped his feet in rhythm to the music he mustered up, and sang for them on perfect pitch, "Please don't step on my blue suede shoes." My grandmother chuckled, and we all joined in laughing from the entertainment from his two-year-old showmanship.

My dad, a former Louisiana Assemblies of God District Secretary-Treasurer, relates this story about Mikey, his only grandson, concerning when he visited them in Alexandria, Louisiana. They lived in a two-story home. Mikey went upstairs, unaccompanied and without their knowledge. He pulled a freestanding, five-foot tall floor lamp next to the window, and proceeded to swing out the window by the lamp cord. When he came crashing to the ground due to the short length of the cord, my dad heard the thud and a cry. The debris from the construction where Dad was adding an office was against the house, and Mikey had landed on the broken bricks.

Running to Mikey's rescue, my dad said, "Son, are you all right?

Mikey said with tears streaming down his face more from aggravation than pain, "If it'd been a rope, I'd ah made it!"

Even though Mikey could have been badly hurt, that was not the case. Dad told the story far and near. Especially, the now famous family phrase: "If it'd been a rope, I'd ah made it."

Reboot now to the backyard, December 22, 1982, when Mikey hit the bowl of burning gasoline with the broom, splashing it in his face and all over his clothing. Instantly he became a blazing fire. After he rolled once on the ground, panicking, he ran around the yard, the blaze growing larger while oxygen fed the conflagration. Next, it seems as if he just appeared in the kitchen where Jean and I were busy mixing ingredients for the delicious pies. I looked up from my baking, and terror shot through me like an arrow that hits its mark. My beautiful son was totally enveloped in flames. His arms were stretched out, his searing flesh hanging off his arms like melting wax. He was making a staccato noise with his lips as one does when he is cold. Mikey was completely on fire—except for his large, deep blue eyes, which were now wide open with fear, pain, and the incredulous stare of disbelief.

Adrenalin rushed through my veins like a jet engine on steroids. I understood how Samson must have felt when he slew the three thousand with the jawbone of an ass. I felt supernaturally endued with abnormal strength and clarity of mind.

Jean threw a towel toward him. I grabbed his body, smothered the flames burning him with my own body, and jerked off his deteriorating shirt. The discarded shirt melted from the heat petroleum-based threads was still standing upright in the corner beside the dining table when we returned home months later. The decals on the shirt melted into one unrecognizable blur like plaster.

The image of my son on fire is permanently ingrained in my mind, my spirit, and my emotions. The shock and sheer terror of the experience will never leave me. When fiery scenes appear on television, like in "The Towering Inferno," I can't watch them. I just can't bear it. Furthermore, it was many years before I could look at a fire burning in a fireplace because that was the height of the flames that melted his flesh.

MIKEY

More chaos ensued as we rushed from the house to the car. I told my mom, "The fire is still going!"

She dashed to where it was burning, turned the water faucet on to it, and left it. I remember thinking so very vividly, *Water doesn't work on that fire.*

MARIGOLD

"There's a fire in the yard," Mikey said with desperation in his voice.

There was a water hose connected to the faucet just outside the back door. I turned the water on and threw the hose toward the fire, not knowing if it reached the fire or not. At that very moment, I could have cared less if the fire burned our house to the ground. One of the key elements that made up the "home" was seriously close to losing his life. I knew it was critical to get him to the hospital. There was no time to call an ambulance. Time meant life; and wasted time meant death.

I said, "Mikey, get in the car. I can't carry you." I couldn't carry him because everywhere I touched his skin; the flesh came off in my hands.

He crawled into the back seat of Jean's blue Mustang, which was the last car in the driveway. I jumped into the driver's seat, started the car, shifted into reverse, and started backing the car up. Jean hurried into the front passenger seat with the car in motion. As a rule, Jean allowed *no one* to drive her car—and I mean *no one*—but I

HAD to drive, and drive quickly. Her faithful friendship forgave my boldness. Pressing down the car horn with all my strength, the raucous blast broke into the deadly silence. As if the very sound of the screaming horn would save us, we raced like a runaway NASCAR blue streak to the hospital emergency room. Before we reached the hospital, the horn burned out.

Stealing a glance at Mikey in the rearview mirror, I asked Jean, "Is that ashes or dirt on his face?"

"Drive, Marigold. Just drive!" Jean urged.

MIKEY

We sped to the hospital. In my mind, I was saying so many things. *I am sorry, Mom, for disobeying. Please don't be mad at me. . . . I am sorry, Miss Jean for getting gross stuff on your car. . . . I am sorry, sorry, sorry.* All that came out, however, was just me sucking in air as wave after wave of hellacious pain destroyed me.

In that moment, somewhere in my mind—it had been drilled into me, "If you are ever in trouble, call on Jesus." I was in trouble. I began saying the name—innocent, scared, overcome—I began saying, "Jesus." The muscles in my body seized, tensed, and contracted with each new second of time as the pain multiplied upon itself. But I said, "Jesus!" Somewhere between home and the hospital, I was filled with the Spirit of God and began to speak in tongues—a language only God understands.

Now you may not believe in such things, or more likely not understand it, and that's fine. The purpose of this testimony is not to be a doctrinal battlefield, but to simply tell you—accurately and honestly—what happened.

When I began to speak in tongues, the waves of pain began to slip out of my awareness. My body still writhed and flexed with obvious response to sheer torment, but my mind calmed. That peace endured and, at times, was my single tether of desire to live in the coming days.

MARIGOLD

Mikey said without any note of panic in his voice, almost a whisper, "Hurry, Mother. Hurry!"

Following these words, a very strange thing happened. Mikey began to softly speak in a heavenly language. He had not previously been baptized in the Holy Spirit. Yet, on this day, with his tongue, face, throat, and his entire upper body burned—and only minutes away from being unable to speak at all—Mikey was calmly baptized in the Holy Ghost, and prayed in a language he had never heard before. He was filled with the Spirit of God on the way to the hospital.

This spiritual miracle was the beginning of God's revelation of His divine presence upon Mikey's life. God has been with our son every step of his journey, entirely trustworthy in the midst of our crisis. We have learned that the Almighty God is worthy of our complete unabated childlike faith known as trust.

When our son relates this story he is fond of saying, in a teasing manner of course, "I survived the fire, and Mom almost killed me on the way to the hospital."

The truth was that my heart was beating so loudly I was sure it could be heard above the Mustang engine. I had a sick feeling of encroaching doom igniting in my gut, creating my own internal fire. It's at times like this that I am especially thankful that I have a relationship with Jesus Christ, and not just a church-going religion.

MIKEY

It is ironic all of the things we take for granted like breathing, the air around us, the joy and warm embrace of the southern states' climate. It is far more ironic when those same things become enemies to your comfort. Imagine searing pain to accompany every breath pulled in, making breathing almost less desirable because of the pain that follows. Imagine the very air surrounding you gaining teeth and beginning to bite every inch of your seared flesh, sending shockwaves through your mind and chest, leading to only thoughts of escape. Imagine the warmth becoming a heat like that of a stoked fire pressed against your exposed muscles, feeling as though you are being roasted for some demonic feast. Was this now my experience, my new life, my future? Nothing was as it should be, and it was all my fault.

MARIGOLD

Mikey and I blasted through the emergency door while Jean parked the Mustang. The flesh on his arms dripped like candle wax hanging in strips a foot long under his arms. It reminded me of an old western jacket my parents had purchased for me on a trip to the famous western town of Dodge City when I was about Mikey's age.

The attending ER nurse entered the room carrying a large bowl of ice with just a small amount of water, and proceeded with the doctor's help to bathe his body with the mixture to control the pain and cool him down.

MIKEY

By the provision and grace of the Lord, I arrived at St. Tammany Parish Hospital. We rushed into the ER and they responded to my desperate fight for life. The immediate response was to place me into a sterile tub with two-thirds ice and water to try to ease the desperate, physical rage my bodily systems were evoking to fight to live. Swelling soon set in, and it lingered. It was an extreme contrast to what I understood to be true. How strange for the cold to be my comfort—like a grave, the cold cocoon of passing was more comfort than to remain. Surely, my young heart could not have toyed with such heavy concepts with any clarity at that time, but as I reflect now, I see things as they were, as they felt, and I can describe them with detail and accuracy.

MARIGOLD

It didn't take a rocket scientist to know when Mike arrived at the hospital. Jean had used a payphone in the hall outside the emergency room to inform him of Mikey's accident. I heard the squealing of wheels as he approached the emergency room area of the small hospital. He abandoned his car at the sliding doors; and, as I recall, it was Jean who parked it for him. The desk nurses just pointed to Mikey's room, for they knew Mike well as pastor. Our church was rather large, and Mike did his own hospital visitation; therefore, he was a regular figure on the premises—someone they referred to as Pastor.

Charging into the room, he was not prepared for what he saw. Mikey's only words to his dad were, "Are you gonna whup me?" This broke Mike's heart. The reason for Mikey's response was due to a conversation earlier that week when Mike had told him never to play with fire. These would be the very last words we would hear him utter for weeks to come. Unbeknownst to us, his throat was already swelling shut due to the fire he had inhaled into his windpipe and lungs!!

MIKEY

My father arrived in the ER. I really struggle to imagine what was going through his mind as he looked down on his son, obviously wounded unto a deadly state. I now have children, and the thought of one of them feeling what I felt or being where I was that day literally crushes my insides. I can't go to that place. What would it have been like to have seen through his eyes, beat with his heart, and bear his emotions in that moment of passing the threshold into that ER room and seeing his boy? I can't imagine; in fact, I should refuse to try to imagine.

Upon seeing him, my first inclination was to settle a childish concern—I asked if he was going to discipline me. It's so humorous now to look back on that moment and realize the obvious innocent repentance. I can't count how many times I was told not to play with fire—to only use such things under the supervision of someone much wiser and more experienced. Oh, had I simply obeyed! It is a dry irony, which causes the mind to whisper the Scriptures' caution of, "Obedience is better than sacrifice," and see for me, at that time, no truer words had ever been uttered. The extent of this sacrifice, this penalty for a moment's foolishness, would become clearer and more burdensome in the following days and years. War had come to Mikey Cheshier; the battles would be fierce, the casualties many, and only a champion for my cause could bring any hope of victory.

To no one's surprise the obvious became clear—I was burned far too badly to receive treatment in any meaningful way at a small town hospital.

Though at this time no one knew the extent of damage the fire had wrought upon my person, that which was visible overwhelmed the staff there. Immediate plans with transit agreement to move me by ambulance to more exacting care at Ochsner Hospital in New Orleans, Louisiana were arranged.

What has to be grasped and understood by those who would read this story is this: the pain, terror, fear, shock, racing heartbeats, chaotic thoughts, and hell on earth was not measured in days, but seconds. Moment by moment these things folded upon themselves, becoming more complex and difficult to field. Not one second passed without multiple elements listed above exacerbating in wrathful force. Not a second! Each moment was measured in degrees of suffering. This condition persisted for days, weeks, months, in some ways years.

MARIGOLD

Mikey was now wrapped in gauze from the top of his head to the toes on his feet. For a while, I could see his shining blue eyes peeping from beneath his mummy wrap. St. Tammany hospital staff had done all that they could do at this point, and now he would be transported to a different medical center located on the far side of New Orleans in a suburb called Metairie on the Mississippi River. None of us, including St. Tammany Hospital emergency room staff, had a clue as to what lay ahead of us, or I feel sure things would have been handled very differently.

The doctor summoned an ambulance to transport Mikey to the New Orleans hospital. Upon arrival, the driver had the nerve to demand payment in advance. I had never heard of such a thing. As a pastor's wife, I had been with many sick or hurt people who required the services of an ambulance, and had never noticed this policy before. I was outraged at the unbelievable temerity of this company to demand we pay at the very moment when our child's situation was so critical. The angry visceral emotion in my gut wanted to read him the riot act, but our energy had to be focused on saving Mikey. We just felt so helpless. Mike took out the checkbook and paid the company as they had demanded.

The emergency room doors opened to the gurney bearing our baby boy wrapped from head to toe in white bandages. He was rolled out and loaded into the back of the ambulance. I quickly crawled in beside him, along with the *attending paramedic*, which later we discover was no paramedic at all. Mike joined the driver/owner of the ambulance company in the front seat for the fifteen-mile drive just to get to the twenty-four-mile long Causeway Bridge that ends in the big city of New Orleans.

MIKEY

Getting to New Orleans from Covington was no small feat at that time. A twenty-three-mile causeway bridge crossing a wasteland of watery nothingness with double spans of a concrete marvel spanning Lake Pontchartrain separated our cities. Depending on traffic, it could take a considerable time to trek. I can easily recall many trips across that bridge just hoping to see something to break up the visual monotony and continual "thump, thump, thump" of the tires on the uneven joints of the bridge.

In transit to New Orleans, I died. In the back of that ambulance, the swelling overcame my breathing space. For the moments that turned into an eternity as that ambulance driver made heroic efforts to get to the hospital—jumping medians, going the wrong way in traffic, and blowing through traffic signals—I lay dead in the back of his vehicle.

Maybe you would love to hear that at this time I had some kind of out of body experience and my spirit chased the ambulance on its heart-racing paths through the "Big Easy." It perhaps would be inspiring if I said some light greeted my passing, and upon following it, I found heaven waiting. These were not my experience with death—a state that greeted me five times within this ordeal. I experienced something far more precious—peace. At the moments of passing the memories are very similar and clear. I remember being liberated from pain and weight. All at once, the pain stopped, the stress stopped, the weight of life left me, and there was in its place comfort. The sensation was a surrounding by a darkness—not a scary darkness, or even an intimidating darkness, but a calming darkness. I liken it to what I imagine a cocoon might be like—surrounded and secure, shut out from the world that has teeth and fire and fear. It was a simple joy. There was in that place a voice of sorts. I can't say if I "heard" that voice or I knew that voice in my spirit, but it said to me, "Wait . . . Wait . . . Okay." This little statement, which to the reader may be meaningless, held such unimaginable comfort to me. This statement meant someone was there, and He had authority over my living and dying, just like a father in complete control and management of that which is his. Following that statement, I was flooded with sensation. The pain, weight, fear, teeth, fire, and suffering once again were full-blown as I returned to life.

I am not trying to discount anyone else's experience that falls within Biblical reason. I am not trying to offer fodder for building a new doctrine or belief. I don't even believe that is the normative experience for those who may pass under suffering. I simply am conveying facts. These facts are: I knew when I died and when I returned to life. There was comfort, peace, and joy awaiting me each time. There was a presence and a voice that greeted me and commanded my moments within these moments. I am certain I was held in comfort—as a baby swaddled tightly held in the arms of its parent—waiting to return to my suffering person. As I said, this experience persisted through each time of death as I recall it. As for now, I am giddy to see what is behind the veil, and what wonders await those who die in Christ.

MARIGOLD

We had just begun our arduous journey onto the bridge when I noticed changes taking place under Mikey's wrappings. His charred flesh was protruding outside of the gauze, and the wrapping that remained in place appeared stretched beyond the breaking point of its ability to hold. He looked as if he was about to explode, much like a balloon being filled with air bound by tape wrapped totally around it—except it was not a balloon being filled up with air; but rather it was my baby boy. Fluids from the body's natural defense of edema filled his cells to ward off this hideous invasion from hell.

I said, "Mikey?" But there was no answer. "Son, can you hear me?"

He neither moved nor spoke. With my heart racing out of my chest, I placed my face to his nose and mouth, searching for some sign of life. Nothing! Nothing at all!!! No air! Nothing at all! Zilch! My heart screamed, *He's dead.Oh God, No, please!* I turned in a panic to the *paramedic* that we had just paid to safely transport our son to a second hospital, and said, "He needs oxygen. He's not breathing. Please Hurry!"

I could have died! I felt my heart almost go into cardiac arrest on the spot when he said, and I quote, "Don't look at me, Lady. I'm just a mechanic." End of quote.

Just for a moment, I imagined pulling his eyeballs out of their sockets, and throwing them back in his head. I would have killed him right then and there, but I knew that my prayers were the only thing that could save Mikey now. I couldn't fuss, beat the man up, and touch God all at the same time. There was no time to waste on anger or unproductive words. I didn't say one word to this fraud who had masqueraded as a paramedic; and I couldn't even let Mike know what was happening, for there was no way of communication from the back to the front. Some ambulance! What a joke!

I knelt on the floor of the ambulance, placing my arm over Mikey's stomach without touching him at all, and began to pray in the Spirit as humbly as I knew how, calling upon the mercies of the Father to do what I did not have the power to do— to save Mikey's life. I allowed the Spirit to pray through me for the situation. God was Mikey's only hope for survival.

The drive seemed as an eternity—an endless grinding of wheels going round and round but getting nowhere. I have never viewed an ambulance the same since that day.

One of the most precious gifts from God—my very heartbeat—was lying in that ambulance, hanging by a thread between life and death. I actually was not sure that he was not already with the Lord. There was no movement or breath coming from his swollen body.

Finally completing the crossing of the Lake Pontchartrain Bridge—the longest continuous span bridge in America—we entered New Orleans. A greater challenge now loomed before us as immediately upon exiting the bridge we found ourselves in a dreadful traffic jam. If I had not been praying so hard for Mikey's life, I would have jumped from the vehicle and demanded all those cars to get out of the way. The drivers showed no respect for the loud siren; they just kept breaking in line resulting in a bigger jam. Our driver, finally realizing that Mikey was fading, if not already departed, pulled upon the grassy median separating the two highways, and drove—dodging signs, bushes, and at times even straddling ditches as necessary.

Finally . . . finally, we reached the Ochsner Hospital, and a team of *real paramedics* rushed Mikey away from us to the emergency intensive care.

MIKEY

Arriving at the hospital with a dead child was not a moment of celebration. Immediately the medical staff sought to revive me, and God oversaw the proceedings as Master of all. He, in His mercy and kindness, saw fit to allow me to live. This marked a turning point that would govern my world for the coming weeks.

The swelling had moved out of control. My eyes swelled shut, my ears swelled shut, my nose swelled, my gums swelled over my teeth, as my head swelled past any natural boundaries. This made all sound, sight, smell, and taste unattainable. One sense was in full force: TOUCH! and every touch was for this period an exercise in torment.

My days were not measured in meals or sunup and sundown. My days were not measured in sleep, as it was hard to tell the difference at times. My days were measured in pain.

Let me try to convey this in some way that you can get a sense of the thoroughness of the suffering. My wounds required individual cleansing and dressing three times a day. For example, my entire right arm would be stripped of skin and scabs; then this highly sensitive local would be bathed in bleach. While I was sitting in this bleach solution, my caregivers took wire brushes, steel wool, and scrubbing pads to peel back all the scabs and damaged tissue. I could not see, or hear their words of remorse and comfort. I existed in this way day after day—my body slowly making its way towards healing.

I am being careful here to only address what I know, and not what I have heard. I have heard many interesting things about this time of my crisis of which I was unaware. It would be less than clear to present someone else's thoughts or ideas during this time as my own, so I have a limited scope of material for a rather large portion of this initial period.

MARIGOLD

Out of sight, gone, swept away in one brisk moment by the attendees. Anguish and pain racked my heart for my baby, and I felt angry that such a thing could have happened in the first place. The pungent scents of alcohol filled the air; nurses scurried down the open corridor toward the doors through which moments before they had rolled my son, leaving me in shock with feelings I couldn't form into words. My emotions were twirling around inside like a tilt-a-whirl. I've never liked tilt-a-whirls! They always cause me to lose the contents of my stomach, and this ride was provoking the same results. Standing there in the middle of the sterile colorless hall, I felt overwhelmed, numb, and powerless to do anything but pray, and the words I prayed seemed to stop just outside my mouth, never reaching heaven. There was such an explosion of painful emotion within me that I wanted to tear the hospital down brick by brick, hit something, break something, or take off running until there was no strength left to run, and just crumble into a heap. I called my mother and dad, our daughter, my sister and brother-in-law, needing to tell somebody, anybody.

Our fourteen-year-old daughter, Melissa, came in the early days. After taking one look at her brother, she turned and ran out of the room, saying, "This is not my brother." He was unrecognizable and completely wrapped in gauze dressings. For a time she lived in denial until one day she sat with him while we went for a bite to eat. Mikey had been a restless child, often keeping us awake at night. Melissa, being seven years older, would pat his back and sing *Away in a Manger,* and at times managed to lull him to sleep. Though she could not touch him, she now began to sing the tune to her baby brother whose eyes were burned shut and appeared to be in a vegetative state lying there in his prison of a bed. She knew it was Mikey when a tear rolled out from his swollen eyes down his cheek.

Concerned it would give her nightmares, I tried to protect Melissa from seeing her brother. She needed to be in school. My mother came for a few days to care for Melissa, but they had obligations and couldn't stay for very long periods. So Melissa moved in with her friend, which at the time seemed the only answer. I was so torn with the dilemma of my separated family. It haunted my mind. I knew Melissa needed me, and Mikey needed me. Each day we thought would be his last.

Over the next number of months, and even years, we came to know God in a way that we had not known Him up to this point in our lives, and it spilled over into our ministries, affecting them for the remainder of our lives.

ANGELS ON ASSIGNMENT

Thank God that He doesn't always answer our prayers in the way we ask. He knows what we need even before we ask. I have learned that when we call upon Him, and we are earnest, He will answer in a way that works for our good, which is the very best for us—not necessarily giving us what we ask. We can only see the present moment, but our sovereign God sees all things from eternity to eternity. That is the reason we can trust Him with our short lives. He is eternal; we are bound in this temporal existence.

Many times I stared out of the hospital room window, like one transfixed, watching the traffic passing on the street eleven stories below, going busily about their daily existence. I silently screamed, *What is so important that they are going to and fro when my world has come to a screeching halt? Don't people understand that my baby is burned, dying, and living in his own personal hell?* The whole business of living, at that moment, seemed all vanity and meaningless. The busyness of the highways reminded me of a colony of African army ants assiduously going this way and that way, seemingly accomplishing little. From my tragedy-focused perspective, nothing mattered except my burned, dying son and his pain.

Day after day, I maintained my vigil of watching the world go by like a forlorn dove from the elevated perch of the pediatric intensive care unit of the hospital. Heartbroken, gut-wrenching feelings of deep sorrow swept over me like ice-laden waves of the ocean relentlessly sweeping the shores of an arctic sea as I helplessly watched my baby boy suffer. Each day I was told that he very possibly would not live to see another. I finally gazed up into the heavens, and said, "Lord, my son is saved, filled with Your Spirit, and ready for heaven. Please don't let him lay here and suffer like this. Please take him home to heaven to be with You where he will suffer no more."

Mike, his dad, alternately paced the halls like a wounded lion when we could not be in the room due to some procedure, or sat by the bed and stared out that eleventh floor window, praying God would preserve our son's life at any cost.

The day the Lutheran pastor from our community walked into the hospital where Mike was pacing and praying to give him a message from God was a turning point for him. Mike laughingly says to this day he was surprised at that because he didn't know that God spoke to Lutherans. This one, however, had been baptized in the Holy Spirit in the Charismatic movement, and was definitely in hearing distance of the Lord. Ray told Mike the Lord had given him the 27th Psalm in the Living Bible, which reads in part, "You shall see the mercy of the Lord in the land of the living." Then Ray and his wife took our hands, creating a small circle in the busy halls of that great hospital with people passing on both sides like waters of a brook gurgling by a stone in the middle, and began to pray in the language of the Spirit. We will forever be so grateful for that wonderful man of God and his lovely wife. For Mike, the issue was settled. No matter how difficult would be the days ahead, our son was going to live.

God heard our prayer. However, the Father in His sovereign purpose did not give me what I asked for. Mikey continued to live in a vegetative state.

God knew something at that point in time I did not know, but was soon to find out for myself. Our Father sees the entire picture, for which I am grateful. My prayer was somewhat like the prayer of Elijah in the Second Book of Kings, when he said, "God, let me die." God heard his prayer, for He always hears our prayers. However, He didn't honor Elijah's prayer any more than He did mine. Rather, He sent angel food cake to Elijah, delivered by the hands of one of His heavenly messengers; and the cake was enough nourishment to carry him all the way to the Mount of God where he found victory. One of the reasons I love this story so much is because it shows how our loving Father watches out for us and gives to us just exactly what we need at the season of need to make it through. I also prayed many times, "God, take Mikey's pain away, be his morphine and valium" (his veins had collapsed from the burns and overuse), "and Lord, would You send angels to play with him? He is just a little boy." God heard and answered that prayer exactly as I had prayed.

Mike continued to try to pastor. On the second Sunday after Mikey's tragedy, Mike felt he needed to make contact with the church. Although I don't think he even knows how he got the strength to do it, he went home and preached from 2 Corinthians chapter 4:8-13 NIV, which says in part, *"We are hard pressed on every side but not crushed, perplexed but not in despair, persecuted but not abandoned, struck down but not destroyed. We always carry around in our body the death of Jesus, so that the life of Jesus may also be revealed in our body. For we who are alive are always being given over to death for Jesus' sake, so that his life may be revealed in our mortal body, So death is at work in us, but life is at work in you. It is written: 'I believed; therefore I have spoken.'*

"With that same spirit of faith we also believe and therefore speak. Because we know that the one who raised the Lord Jesus from the dead will also raise us up with Jesus, and present us with you in his presence. All this is for your benefit, so that the grace that is reaching more and more people may cause thanksgiving to overflow for the glory of God. Therefore, we do not lose heart. Though outwardly we are wasting away, inwardly we are being renewed day by day. For our light and momentary troubles are achieving for us an eternal glory that far outweighs them all. So we fix our eyes not on what is seen, but on what is unseen. For what is seen is temporary, but what is unseen is eternal" (vv. 13-18).

As for me, I don't even remember going home to pack. I'm sure friends gathered things for me from time to time. Mike and I held little comfort for each other. When he held me, I could feel his pain rushing through me, adding to the incredible pain that was racking my whole being. We were a bit like trying to put two magnets together by attaching the negative poles together. Anyone knows they tend to repel instead of adhere. I was going about the motion of living, but feeling absolutely dead inside. At times I wanted to tear the hospital down brick by brick, throw something—anything—to release the built-up tsunami that was raging within my soul.

But I did none of those things. I turned to the only One who has the power to save, and fell into His oceans of mercy.

MIKEY

After about one month I began to have sounds and sights return as the swelling began to lessen. Not all at once, mind you, but little by little. I began to see faces, and I began to return into the world of the living through the doors of the rest of my senses. Sounds began to come, words of comfort and calm. I heard my name. The voice was familiar; it was my mother. I heard another voice—my father. I began to hear things that brought me from a dark place where only occasional visits from the Divine broke up the focus on pain. I remember sight was like looking through slits and barely able to make things out. This was the world I wanted to be in; this was the one I missed. I struggled to see, to hear, to speak—I still couldn't speak. My eyelids were barriers, and I needed to move them. They were in the way. I strained against them—as a strong man straining at the weight of an object too heavy for his person, I strained. I strained to escape this place of loneliness, to trade it for a place with people and without pain. I had no idea there would be no escape, but a reality—a reality so cold and brutal so as to make me to wonder if death were not the wiser goal.

Were you to take a photo album and flip through it, images of moments would greet you. I personally like pictures more than video in many ways—a picture captures more of the imagination. A video, oftentimes, leads to a tremendous letdown, and fills in all the blanks with the monotony of progression. However, a well-timed and composed picture allows the viewer to let his imagination conceive the remains in a personal way. Let me take you through some snapshots of my earliest visual memories after my sightless journey.

I lay in a room in a bed with white and brown bandages covering most of my body. A stuffed animal is there—a puppy with a bulbous head and droopy eyes as if to sympathize with my plight. On this puppy were stains of different hues of blood and oozing. It appeared to me as if someone had attempted to clean it several times. The bandages were not all clean, as in some places there had been a breach by whatever they were trying to protect. I couldn't move well. The room was small and sterile in its fixtures. A fluorescent light shone over the bed, and I recall a lot of connections protruding from me. There was a connection at the base of my neck, a light blue or white-ridged tube that carried air to me with a hiss and moist sound. The mist choked me, and I wanted it to go away, but couldn't ask for or do it myself.

"Get Well Soon" pictures or notes were on the wall. As I remember it, there were many supporting cards and coloring book pages from other children and such. I remember many of these in a collage of sorts on a wall or window. I now find it humorous to imagine the idea of getting "well." What would that idea even look like? Would in some instant it all be over, and I become well? Would the wounds disappear? Would the pain be forgotten? Would the terror be unlived? Would it all just be as if it never was? How could I become well? There was no going back, and there was no initial peace; there was only adaptation and recovery to something completely different. I was not well, and perhaps would never be fully well again. I understand the loving intentions behind every card and note. I understand how the desire to comfort compelled the pen to write, but how could "well" ever be known again? My face and chest and lungs and innocence and life had been ravaged by one cursed match; and the effects of those things would ultimately set the elements in place for the construction of someone and something completely different than what had been before. Those humble pieces of paper—fluttering at the corners when someone passed by, discolored by marker, crayon, pencil, and pen—held a tease in their secret places—a tease of being well.

As bleak as this seems, it was not to be my thoughts for long. A day would soon come when perspectives would become something entirely different, and in the most unusual of ways.

I recall waking from darkness to lights dimmed for my benefit. The truth is, one really wouldn't enjoy seeing in any real clarity of light the things that were around you. The nasty bandage changes—with caretakers trying to pick out the strands of linen as flesh grew around them in between changes—were not visually pleasant.

Some of my earliest images upon seeing again were of the scrub room. I remember a place of hard edges and cold metal—a stainless steel tub where they placed me in bleach water. All faces were covered by breathing masks; all heads were covered with paper caps; all the hands were covered in rubber gloves. I saw only the eyes. Now, I sympathize with these folk who had the task of saving children's lives by peeling away their flesh. I can't imagine the exercises one must do to make your hands continue to inflict pain when the child is screaming. The screams in that place were constant. The nurses' eyes were all flat and without sparkle. Occasionally one would "smile" with his eyes in order to convey some sympathy for the suffering, but then go right back to stripping your skin from you. The decorations were sparse with various instruments of pain infliction—like a sterile torture chamber to be sure not to kill the victim being terrorized. With several stations available, several kids could be dealt with at a time. After being completely cleansed of the dead flesh and scabbing, the patient was lifted out and placed onto a table colored a deep orange by the heat lamps to dry. Towels were avoided for fear of leaving some tiny piece of fabric behind in a wound, and thereby infection finding a root to grow. This was my routine—the images that greeted me—the bloody, painful, overwhelming process of healing.

Pictures of this time are grizzly and painful to remember. These images were not for a day or two; they continued for weeks. I could go into really horrible stories—the kind of stories that make you grit your teeth and suck in air, leaving you thankful it wasn't you—but I will not for your sake, and, I am hopeful, you are only having a taste of the suffering instead of a stomach full.

MARIGOLD

Three times a day, the scabs that formed on Mikey's burns were scrubbed off with steel wool and bleach. This procedure was done in a sterile room where tubs and equipment made it look more like a torture chamber than a room for healing. We named this the debriding room as this was its purpose. We accompanied his gurney as far as the swinging doors of this area; then they continued down the long sterile hall where Mikey was taken for this agonizing procedure. We waited by the doors until he was rolled back through some three hours later. His veins had collapsed, and he had nothing to dull the pain of these scrubbings.

One day, as Mikey was being wheeled from a debriding procedure, just as his gurney entered the corridor where we were allowed to stand, I thought I heard a faint whisper escaping his lips. It had been almost a month—the night of his accident—since we had heard him speak.

"Stop the gurney, I think he's trying to say something," I said.

The attendants immediately stopped dead in their tracks, and the hall became silent as I placed my ear to Mikey's charred lips, and stood motionless. Straining, I heard a breathy whisper, "Mom, you know why I have not died from the pain? I heard the doctors tell you that could happen."

I said, "No, son, tell me why you have not died from the pain."

With my ear as close as I dared get to his burned mouth, he once again spoke in a soft, breathy whisper—almost too faint to hear, "Because I have not felt any pain. Angels have come and played with me every day, even Michelle." God had answered my prayer!!!

Standing in the hall beside my son's gurney, with tears flowing like an opened river dam, I began to sing the old storied hymn of the church, "Great Is Thy Faithfulness." The attendees stood there with Mikey until I finished my song of praise to Jesus, my Lord.

Mikey had said angels, even Michelle, had come and played with him. Michelle was my sister's only child who had died of adult acute leukemia five short years before, at ten years of age. Michelle was a loving child who often rocked and played with Mikey when she visited. He loved her dearly. Her death had rocked our entire family, and challenged our faith. She had insight that many who live to a ripe old age never learn, and was a testimony to all who knew her. Two weeks before her home-going, she selected the song "Whatever It Takes," and asked me to sing it at her funeral.

When Marcia, her mother, said, "Don't talk like that; we are believing God for your healing," she said, "Everyone is healed—some in this life, and some when they get to heaven. Some are healed in heaven, and some on earth." She possessed wisdom far beyond her years on spiritual matters.

I sang for her celebration of eternal life as I had promised her I would, although it was one of the hardest things that I've ever done.

Had Mikey been in heaven some of this time with his cousin and an angelic host, or had God sent His heavenly host to Mikey? I guess the answer to that question we will never know until we reach heaven, and then it probably won't matter. One thing I know for sure: God had been Mikey's morphine, valium, and any other pain medicine that he had need of, and had sent angels on a special assignment to minister joy to him. And one of those visiting angels was Michelle, his cousin, who was already with the Lord on the other side of the veil.

Yes, God had heard my prayer for deliverance, and He chose to answer in His way—the best way. He was taking care of Mikey all along. He never once left him alone to suffer. After all, Mikey belonged to Jesus. I was fond of saying that Mikey was a *Jesus baby*. God saw the whole picture. God had a bigger plan for Mikey; a plan to put steel in his soul; a plan for Mikey's good and not evil. The devil had intended this to destroy Mikey, but God was turning it for His good. It is so comforting to know that God has got it all under control.

MIKEY

Spiritually, wonders were accomplished. In the natural as we peered into the reality of our life, mine was over. There was not a silver lining; there was not a rainbow's end to chase; and there was certainly no way for getting back to the way things used to be. In the realm of the divine, however, God was moving at a fever pitch, shoring up my heart with peace, ministering to my soul and mind. He loved on my person moment by moment. I was moved toward emotional adulthood at the speed of light—His light. Several evidences of this transformation could be outwardly observed, but one particular moment stands out.

It was late at night, and all through the burn ward, not a nurse was stirring, but I was awake. I could not sleep, and was becoming a bit more mobile. Up to this point, one of my pastimes was to pull staples out of my grafts as swelling began to go down. There was not always a lot to do lying flat on your back. On several occasions, I had asked for a mirror, but was denied. This night there was a drive in me to see the forbidden.

I eased out of my bed, grasped my IV cart, and shuffled myself into the bathroom attached to my room. I believe the staff was unaware that I could actually get out of bed. Upon arriving in the restroom, I noted a large mirror tilted just so for any handicapped person in need to make use of it—positioned precisely to look this child in the face—the face everyone had been so careful not to let me see. I peered into the looking glass and saw an unfamiliar person. There was a disfigured person with deep wounds staring back at me. It was a scary face, tinged with pain, and it screamed of the suffering it had gone through. That image called out to me. It resonated with my soul. I looked into the eyes of that horrible vision, and reality set in: Those are my eyes. It is me. For a length of time, I stood and looked at the edge of each wound. Every difference! All of it! How it created shapes on my skin. This is me! I remember at that moment a truth cemented in my head—unavoidable and undeniable: This is the aftermath of a miracle! This is what Jesus allowed me to look like, and this is how I will accept it.

I became something of a difficulty after this moment because there were always discussions of plastic surgery, corrective surgery, and how everyone wanted to help me look better, which I adamantly, even aggressively, denied. I looked how I looked, and Jesus was the One who saved me to look like this. If He wanted me to look different, then I would have looked different. This truth anchored in my heart, soul, and mind at seven years of age.

I think now what a profound clarity God gave, and it marked a walk with God that has continued on to this very day. I have a closeness and a friendship that cannot be grasped by the very vast majority of His people, much less those who are not. This was an awakening to service that would overshadow the whole of my life, and give me opportunities to live in ways people only dream about in fanciful thoughts of grandeur. I was free, and I was the product of a miracle.

MARIGOLD

JOY UNSPEAKABLE AND FULL OF GLORY

His mercies were tested on a daily basis. On one such day, I was so desperate to touch God for help. I was at the end of my proverbial rope, and I couldn't tie a knot in it because the end of the rope was in shreds. To say I was empty and my heart was cast down within me was an understatement. I could barely frame the words as I knelt on the cold floor in the tiny bathroom connected to the waiting area where we sat wrestling with our worries over the agony our son was enduring during one of his daily debridings. I rested my head on the white porcelain tub that I had now claimed for an altar. "Help me, Lord," I whispered. "Help!" I didn't know what to say or how to pray. I was too distraught to quote any scriptures. From the depths of sorrow, too painful for words, my spirit cried out from an empty well, "Help."

It is most difficult to explain in words just how low I was on this day. God looked down upon the pitiful scene in that bathroom, and took mercy once again on His lowly servant. He began to pour His joy into my spirit. I could feel myself filling up like an empty tank thirsty for gasoline, unable to move without it. God was filling me up with His presence.

My sorrow began to slowly drift away, and God's presence took its place. But it didn't stop there. I had been running on empty for so long. I was dry, like an old discarded sponge. I drank and drank in His presence like a dying desert creature, until it began to fill my soul. The presence of the Lord began to turn into joy. Not just joy, but a joy unspeakable, unexplainable, indescribable, and full of the glory of the Lord. I was simply so full that I began to weep for joy. Soon I was on my feet, hands raised toward heaven. No longer was this room cold and stale. The room that I had claimed as a prayer closet was now full of the comforting *shekinah* glory of God that had filled me up and was flowing out upon everything around it. My personage could not contain such joy and remain still. I began to jump for joy, and the next thing I knew, the tiny room could no longer hold me. I came into the waiting room dancing and jumping for joy; not mine of my own doing, but a joy that God in His mercy had chosen to give me.

Truly as the psalmist said, "In [His] presence is fullness of joy at [HIS] right hand there are pleasures forevermore" (Psalm 16:11 NKJV).

The painful days rocked on through Christmas and well into the New Year. God had become a great source of strength to me. He placed a reserve inside of me that never seemed to run dry. When I couldn't take the pain anymore, He would step in and give me a drink of fresh living water, joy unspeakable, and full of glory.

The sign on Mikey's isolation ward said: "Parents: 5 Minutes Visiting Time." Mike and I were there around the clock, only leaving to step into a nearby room for a few hours of rest.

One day, Mike asked the nurse, "Why do you allow us to stay for hours on end when the sign on the door clearly says, 'Parents: 5 Minutes Visiting Time'?"

She said, "Because you and your wife are a help. This sign is for the parents' sake who just can't stand to see someone they love in this shape."

Mike and I both knew that the strength we possessed was not ours, but our God's, that He had so mercifully imparted to us when we needed Him the most. He said, "I am an ever-present help in time of trouble" (Psalm 46:1b NIV). His mercies are new every morning, and without them, we would be completely consumed. He said, "I will never let you suffer above that which you are able to bear. In your weakness I am made strong."

I looked into Mikey's deep ocean blue eyes, trying to communicate with eye contact by looking hard and long to see if I could read what he might be thinking. The edema had gone down just enough for him to open his eyes slightly. Even though the eyebrows and eyelashes had been completely burned off, he still had the most beautiful eyes. They had always expressed compassion, tenderness, and love. The doctor had many times prepared us for him to die; and if by some chance Mikey lived, the doctor said that Mikey would probably be blind because his face and upper body were burned the deepest. The last time I had viewed those beautiful eyes, he was engulfed in flames. Now those ocean blues were all I could see—wide and weary from the battle of struggling for one more day of life in the land of the living.

Mikey's bed was located in a single room at the end of a many-bedded intensive care ward. His was the only glassed-in room completely shut off from everyone and everything. They called it reverse isolation—a place to keep you protected from the outside world rather than keeping the outside world from you. Each time we entered his room, we went through a ritual of scrubbing with special scrub brushes and germ killer. After scrubbing up, we put on hairnets, robes, gloves, and shoe covers—much as a surgeon prepares to enter an operating room.

Mikey's veins had collapsed just minutes after each cut down (a surgical procedure to reach a major blood supply below the surface of the skin). This translated into the fact that he had nothing for pain. He was intubated with a breathing tube. His face looked like a basketball due to the edema, and his ears looked like baseballs. From the first day that he arrived in emergency, the surgeons prepared us for the possibility of his ears falling off, and a strong possibility he would lose his nose as well. Brain damage, due to the length of time of oxygen deprivation during the ambulance ride from St. Tammany Parish hospital, was expected if he survived. All the options were bad. All the outcomes were heartbreaking. For the next couple of weeks, the doctors tried to graft skin to his ears, but charred flesh left no blood flow. We helplessly watched as he fought to live in spite of all the hurdles and obstacles to be overcome.

About a week after Mikey had been admitted to Ochsner Hospital, one day a nurse walked into his room and said, "It's time to extubate him; he must learn to breathe on his own." She turned to our son and began pulling the tubes from his throat that the emergency room attendees had put in place the night he was burned. When she finished, she turned and walked out of the room to her desk post just outside his room.

Mikey had not yet spoken. His eyes bugged open looking straight at me as if to say, HELP ME!!

I rang the nurse and she said, "Don't worry he has to learn to breathe on his own."

I glanced back at Mikey as his chest swelled high as if exploding, his eyes rolled back in his head, and his lungs collapsed. I ran out the door past the uninterested nurse and out of the ward into the hall for help. I saw an African American nurse walking toward me. Running to her, I said, "Please help me! My son has died! He can't breathe! Somebody must do something!"

She ran down the hall through the doors to his ward, straight past the nurse, and burst into Mikey's room. For all the world, Mikey looked dead. I felt it had taken too long, and I had surely failed him.

"Oh dear God, help us!" I wailed.

When the attending nurse walked into the room, the nurse I had brought in barked orders like a general in the military, "Get her out of here," (meaning me) "He's gone. . . . Bring me a trach tray . . . NOW!!!"

I left the room with more emotion than a heart should have to feel. There was a bathroom by the nurses' station next to Mikey's room. Sure that Mikey had passed, I pulled the lid down over the toilet, knelt down, buried my face over the lid, and sobbed.

Satan came to me; yes, Satan! Could I see him? No. Could I hear him? Loud and clear! He said, "Tell God you'll never serve Him, preach another message, write another song about Him if this is the way He treats His children."

I said aloud, "And who will I serve? You? I hate you! . . . You did this to my boy, and if I lose everything I have, I will not serve you." I continued my sobbing in peace.

Someone quietly opened the bathroom door, and fell to her knees beside me. It was the African American nurse I had desperately summoned for help. She put her arm around my waist and said, "Someone in heaven must want this boy to live. He was gone! I am the head of respiratory for this entire hospital. I don't even know why I was on this floor; my office is on the third floor. No one else had the authority to do what I did. I opened a hole in his throat, and put in a breathing tube. Your son is alive."

My heart leaped for joy! I wasted no time hugging her neck and racing to Mikey's side.

As days turned into weeks, and weeks into months, no one seemed to put two and two together to realize that Mikey was as badly burned on the inside as on the outside. After many attempts to extubate (remove the breathing tubes) failed, the doctors finally came to the conclusion that Mikey's throat was fused together, making it impossible for air to pass through. In short the prognosis was he would wear a metal breathing tube, a trach, for the remainder of his life. A tracheotomy (trach) tube is a curved tube that is inserted into a tracheotomy stoma (the hole made in the neck and windpipe, technically known as the trachea).

Our tracheostomy tube consisted of three parts: outer cannula with flange (neck plate), inner cannula, and an obturator. The outer cannula is the outer tube that holds the tracheostomy open. A neck plate extends from the sides of the outer tube, and has holes to attach cloth ties to wrap around the neck and hold it firmly in place. The inner cannula fits inside the outer cannula. It locks to keep it from being coughed out, and is removable for cleaning. The obturator is used to insert a tracheostomy tube. It fits inside the tube to provide a smooth surface to guide the tracheostomy tube as it is inserted.

After time, when the canal of his neck became firm, the doctors did away with the outer tube, and had us insert a single tube directly into his neck. He had no control of liquid or blood oozing from the trach.

After the trach was in place, there was nothing more that could be done for his air passage. One day while still at Ochsner Hospital in New Orleans, he started struggling for air. Once again it looked as if Mikey could no longer draw a breath. Mike and I began to pray fervently. A large blood clot shot like a bullet out of his trach to the opposite side of the room, landing fixed in the middle of the wall. That's when the suction of his lungs became a ritual. I could hardly believe it as charred flesh, blood clots, and ash was suctioned from his lungs and breathing passage on a regular basis.

During these dark days, it was documented that Mikey quit breathing on five different occasions. At times, he had crossed over to the other shore, but God was not finished with his life. Since all of this had happened during the month that he was being treated at Ochsner Hospital, we realized that Ochsner was not well enough equipped to handle a burn as serious as Mikey's. A representative from Shriners Burns Hospital for Children in Galveston, Texas, approached us about transporting Mikey to their hospital. The Shriners provided a private plane and a physician on the flight with him and the two of us. Mikey would remain in a bed the entire time. They covered all the cost. At this time, we had over $100,000 in bills at Ochsner, and they seemed clueless as to what to do for him. Upon hearing that Shriners had approached us concerning our son's care, the primary doctor told Mike and I that he would pay the entire bill if we would allow Mikey to remain. They needed to learn more about burns as they were opening a burn unit.

First Mike's neck went red, and the redness continued upward as he calculated his words carefully. "Doctor, I know that you have done what you can to help our son, but you will not use him as a test animal. If I have to work five jobs for the rest of my life to pay this bill, then I will, but I'm not leaving him here. Marigold and I are taking him to the burn hospital in Galveston where burns are what they specialize in, and it's all they do."

Needless to say, the doctor was not happy, and charged us fully.

My mind reeled with apprehension of what could happen to Mikey in his fragile physical state during a flight; but at the same time, an acute thrill of anticipation of real help for him was there. We gave thanks to God for His tender love and care as we watched the hall and doorway from Mikey's hospital room, eagerly awaiting the arrival of his new transport.

Two strapping middle-aged men entered Mikey's room with a transport gurney. Gingerly they moved him and his gear onto his new interim mode of transportation and wheeled him to an ambulance. The ambulance transferred Mikey across New Orleans to a flying ambulance—a Cessna 182, piloted by the very kind volunteers of Shriners Institute. This time Mike and I both were beside him with a doctor keeping close vigil who knew how to use the equipment. They lifted the bed into the aircraft, and clamped it to the floor. The aircraft moved forward on the airstrip, slowly at first, and then it picked up the speed needed to lift off the ground. With my eyes fixed on Mikey as we began the flight to Galveston, my lips were engaged in prayer to God for His protection. Mikey was breathing. Thank God, he was breathing.

A child about one year old was with us on the flight. Her mother had purposely stood her in scalding water. She had lost her little toes. Tears rolled down my face as I ached for the child and felt anger toward her mother who was accompanying her. How someone could actually cause this horrible pain and alter a child's life forever, I will never understand. I would have taken my son's place if it were possible.

When we arrived at the hospital, Mikey was placed in a ward with four other burned children. One boy's buttocks and back were severely burned when his cousin—thinking it would be funny—lit a pack of firecrackers while they were still in his pocket. Another boy's eyes had been blown out of their sockets when someone threw a firecracker that hit him in the eyes. One child was burned over ninety percent of his body in a house fire that began in the garage when the hot water heater ignited a gasoline can; he never left the hospital. Mike managed to get a peek at him on one occasion; the only part of his body that had not been burned was in the location of his underwear.

MIKEY

At times during my stay, other children were there. One named Tony was in the bed next to me. He had been right next to a radiator when it exploded, blowing his chest and abdomen open, and searing the flesh. A plastic translucent pad, like a hydrocolloid dressing that you could see through, was used to cover his wounds. I remember seeing Tony's insides. Tony did not survive.

MARIGOLD

The Galveston burn hospital operated in a completely different manner than Ochsner Hospital. In New Orleans we stayed with Mikey around the clock, but that was not allowed at Shriners. We were only allowed to be with him a short time each day—something like thirty minutes or so—in the morning, and about the same amount again in the afternoon. The thought of him suffering alone in his room was almost unbearable for my mother's heart. I wanted to beg and plead to stay. What if he couldn't breathe? Who would run for the nurse? What if he needed pain meds? He surely would feel lonely, overwhelmed, and alone in his pain and suffering. He could barely speak a whisper. *Oh God*, I cried, *I can't leave him. Please help me.* I did not like this rule of Shriners concerning visiting hours, and they absolutely adhered to it. It took the strength of God to get us through the time of separation.

And as always, He was our strong tower into which the righteous run and are safe. Even though being separated from my baby boy for even one minute broke my heart to the point of utter despair, the real truth: this was the first modicum of relief we had had in over thirty days. We moved from the crushing pressure of 24/7 suctioning his trach to keep him from smothering to death, helping care for his wounds because we knew more about these things than most of the nursing corps, and enduring the constant odor of charred flesh trying to heal olfactory assault . . . to walking into a room with our boy bathed, wrapped in clean gauze material, and smelling good. It was truly grace in action.

Many times when we drove onto the hospital parking lot and opened our door, we heard cries drifting across the air from the suffering souls inside. Burn pain is almost unbearable. Sometimes people fall into unconsciousness, which is the body's way of handling it. At times the sounds emanating from the burn wards sounded like the distant cries from the pit of hell.

Unlike some of the other patients, our Mikey had nothing for pain. I said to myself, "Hell was made for the devil and his imps, not my precious little boy." My heart broke into a million pieces. I wished this whole scenario was a bad horror movie happening to someone else, and I was just an understudy—a fill in, if you will—in this soul wrenching drama. This surely had not happened to OUR son, to HIS life, to ALL our lives. Something of this magnitude only happens in the movies.

Each day before leaving Mikey's room, I reminded him of Whose he was. "Mikey," I said, "you belong to Jesus. Never forget that. You are never alone. Jesus is with you every minute of every day. You are a Jesus baby."

As the words fell from my lips, I silently prayed that Jesus would make Himself real to Mikey—to make the veil of flesh very thin between the spirit world where He dwelt, and the natural world where all this pain existed, and comfort him during his suffering. It is still true that in HIS presence there is fullness of joy, which is not contingent on circumstances even in the midst of suffering. In the natural, every minute was so hard. We could have not made it without God.

I've often asked, "What do people do that don't know the Lord?" During our hard time, I learned what some of those who do not know Him do. Some stayed drunk. One lady went out looking for men—any man—to give her a few moments of sensory pleasure, and anesthetize her pain. My heart broke for those who suffered such emotional anguish without Jesus, and I tried to be a witness to them. At the same time, while my heart was broken over the suffering of my son, my Comforter and Deliverer Jesus Christ was with Mikey and me. Of this, I was completely confident.

Finally, the day rolled around, about sixty days after he was burned, when the doctors felt Mike and I should be trained in the procedure of sterile trachea tube changing, and how to debride the constant returning scabs on his burn wounds. If he was not debrided several times a day, sepsis could set in and cost him his life. I soon became a wound care specialist.

Our training session was set. We were very anxious as we walked into the chamber where all the burn patients were treated. It looked more like a torture chamber rather than a treatment room. Metal tubs large enough to accommodate full-grown men were situated near metal tables where the patients were to lie. The three large male African American nurses designated for Mikey's wound care met us at the door.

After a few days of treatments, one of them said, "I have a question for you. What does your son have that none of the other patients have?"

I queried, "What do you mean?"

"Well," the man continued, "we know that he had nothing for pain because of his collapsed veins; yet he acted as if he felt no pain. He splashed us with bleach, wanting to play with us, and even tried to scrub his own burns with a brush. There is something different about this boy. We were anxious to meet you and inquire from you what makes the difference."

Tears swelling in my eyes, I said, "He is a Jesus baby. He has never come into this room alone. Jesus has come with him every time. He belongs to Jesus. He's a Jesus baby!"

I closed my eyes and thanked God for His protection over Mikey. When we could not be there to comfort him, our loving Lord was there. Once again, Jesus was his morphine. Jesus was his Friend. Jesus was his Comforter. Thank You, God, for Jesus.

We painstakingly learned over a period of about three days how to debride Mikey's body, and how to change his trach in a sterile fashion. It was all so intimidating, feeling the overwhelming responsibility for our son's very breath.

I said, "Okay, what do we do if this fails? What do we do if we do it wrong? Where do we go for help if this hole in his neck closes for any reason?

His answer stunned Mike and me, and caused us to pause, leaving us trying to breathe ourselves.

"You will know more about this trach when you leave this hospital than an emergency room doctor."

That was scary and not comforting in any sense of the word. Just the thought of the responsibility made my stomach churn and my head hurt.

"Oh God," we beseeched Him, "how can we do this? We must have Your help."

And so began the mind- and body-wearying saga of the next seven-and-a-half years that Mikey had a metal tube in his trachea with Mike and I being his sole caregivers. At least twice a day, a clean sterile trach was inserted into his neck—even more often during allergy season when heavy drainage could and did clog it up. If the narrow quarter-inch hole in his neck was obstructed for any reason, Mikey became oxygen starved, and could die from the lack of air. These trach tubes had to be boiled continually for sterilization. One needed to be ready to switch out at all times.

MIKEY

I was in the hospital ninety-one days in total from accident to release, although it felt much, much longer—from late December to late March.

We went home: this was a concept that seemed so foreign to me at this time. What is taken for granted by most became a moment of tremendous achievement; I went home. I was so hopeful as I walked through the door that somewhere in the refuge I had always known, there would be peace. . . .

Instead, a dead Christmas tree greeted me. There it was. Like stepping into a time warp, life had been utterly on hold while I died in the hospital. The tree adorned in shiny bulbs and lights was utterly brown and pitiful—any of its former glory consumed. I knew how the tree felt. A banner hanging over the tree on the wall said, "Welcome Home." Though I never asked, I think I was intended to see it much sooner than my eyes fell on it. As I recall, the tree basin was green and red metal with screws fastened into the tree to hold it upright, covered by a velvet skirt. On top of that were our Christmas presents covered in dead pine needles. The tree had shed itself all over the presents, covering them with its death, so that regardless of how hard they tried to shine, death was in the way. Life was so strange; all the facades I had lived behind removed. We tried so hard to pretend the tree lived, still filling our house with its pine scent, but a tinge of rot was mixed in; the colors were meant to distract us from reality, at least for a season. I held in bandage-covered hands presents wrapped with the glamorous paper meant to overshadow the truth of it, which only lasts until life pushes against it. It was all tarnished and dead and brown. I lived in a real world with all the twinkle of fantasy burned off by a terrible tragedy.

To be honest, and outside of this testimony, which I have never really shared before, Christmas is a really difficult time for me. I don't like the presents and the lights and the false pretenses. I live in a real world—one of pain and memories and loss. I long for a day when I am with Jesus, the True Gift. These things are a pitiful substitute for His luster. If I have heard it once, I have heard it dozens of times from my precious family, "Don't be a scrooge."

I have never shared the reasons why: Christmas is a dead tree waiting for me with presents covered in pine needles; and smiles, if only for a moment, try to pretend that pain isn't lurking outside the door. To try to be normal after dying at Christmas has never felt right to me. My first sight upon walking back into my home after the months of hospital nightmare was a reality that nothing could or would ever be the same. Much as the man behind the curtain in the story from The Wizard of Oz, when I pulled the curtain aside to reveal him, he was a terrible man, and his name was Life.

I stepped into my room as it had been left on the day I had idiotically set myself on fire. It now seemed as someone else's room—this room belonged to a boy who had died—no longer full of my interests, but his.

So many restless nights played out in this place. My precious parents had to be vigilant over me, as my tracheotomy was my only way to breathe. Night after night, I woke without breath as if a giant sat on my chest not allowing me to breathe. The trach would flex against my neck as I tried to breathe. I had a bell to ring to wake my parents. They got out of bed and rushed to my room to engage my suctioning machine by taking a ten-inch tube and shoving it through the blockage in my neck to give me air. That tube, shaped to pierce, punched the blockage through to my esophagus, wracking my body with intense pain. At once, my breath returned—fast and labored as the oxygen levels returned to normal. Lying in bed drowning . . . every night . . . for years. This was my plight, my blessing of life.

As I write this, every muscle in my back aches. I have trouble focusing. I must type fast because I want to run away from this memory. Its pain is as vivid today as it ever was. The terror still grips me, though suppressed deep down. It awakens horror unmatched by any demon in hell. I have met some, so I can speak with a degree of authority here. I can't imagine how my parents survived this; I have no clue. There were weeks without sleep, like having a newborn infant requiring your attention every little while as, for six years, you begged for sleep and rest. They rarely let their suffering show, but I know it was there. I saw the dark circles and fear and weariness. They were in a hell, too—different, but intense. That trach was a bear, and it was relentless in its efforts to destroy any blessing my life could be.

I am determined to be clear here: there were, and have been, exceedingly dark moments in life, and though I am well in spirit, mind, and body, it isn't for lack of memories or reasons to rage . . . it is because I don't awaken those terrible things with meditation; and Jesus' love and acceptance has overshadowed it all. I would not have you believe there is no more pain; only that His love is simply stronger. I have not visited some thoughts and memories penned here . . . ever at will. I do this now because Jesus deserves His glory, and someone may find hope herein.

MARIGOLD

Once we brought him home, we had several trachs for changing out of his neck two or three times a day or anytime necessary. He had no control of the mucus discharge that came through his trachea. Many times a day, we had to suction the trachea in order to keep his only breathing passageway clear. When at last, approximately a year after his initial burn, I took him to public school for one hour one day a week, I sat in the principal's office with my suction machine ready to jump into action at the first sign of trouble.

Mikey was outfitted with a rubber mask molded to the contour of his face, with which, although we never saw anything but a couple of advertisements during certain seasons of the year, he looked a little like the *Jason* character in the movie *Halloween*. Over the mask, he wore a tight-fitting elastic Jobst garment that velcroed down the back of his head. It was hot, miserable, and smothering to him. The idea was to place enough pressure on his burn scars to keep them from developing keloid scars—scars that don't know when to stop, or tough heaped-up scar tissue that rises abruptly above the rest of the skin. It usually has a smooth top and a pink or purple color. Keloid scars are irregular in shape, and tend to progressively enlarge. Unlike other normal scars, keloid scars do not subside over time. Mikey had first, second, and third degree burns on his face as well as skin grafts from his legs which served his mischievous side well as he would point to the graft from his thigh and say, "Give me a kiss." He often says he wished they had taken the option of taking the skin from his hip cheek. With a trach in his neck, and Jobst compression garments on his face and arms, moving around was quite the task for him. He developed computer gaming skills before there were any really sophisticated games. His choices were "Frogger," "Pac-man," and the like.

The skin is the largest organ in the body. It is also one of the most important. The skin performs essential functions like temperature regulation, hydration, and protection against invading bacteria. Burn wounds open the way for many bacteria to enter like an invisible invading terrorist army. The regenerative power of skin is no match for the results of the hellish fury of fire. One of the biggest challenges burn care specialists face is to get the body covered again—even resorting to pig skin, which is the closest to human flesh—to conserve the skin of the patient, of which there is only so much. The pain of a severe burn is almost unimaginable—and so is the destruction it causes. The truth is simply this: the body won't last very long without the skin's protection. Large, open wounds are highly susceptible to bacterial infections referred to as sepsis. If these minions from the invisible realm reach the bloodstream, death soon follows.

Another serious condition caused by skin loss is the inability to regulate the body's temperature and hydration to prevent shock. The best treatment option for a severe burn is a skin graft. Skin grafts sound like something straight out of a medieval torture chamber, but skin grafts save lives. To perform a skin graft, surgeons remove healthy skin from a patient's body, and attach it to the wounded area. Extensive scarring is inevitable, and the healing process can be long and painful if the patient survives.

Mikey endured many surgeries to cover his now missing flesh. Large blocks of skin were taken from his legs, stretched to three times their size, and grafted onto his arms, ears, and face. When the doctor asked him if he wanted to use the skin from his buttock or leg for the replacement skin for his face, he put his finger over his trach and said, "You had better use my leg. One day when I have a girlfriend, I can point to my face and say, 'Would you like to kiss my leg?' That just sounds better than the alternative." We all laughed. We had a choice to laugh or cry, and we chose laughter. He had grafts while at Ochsner and Shriners hospitals. He refused plastic surgery on his facial scars.

Desperately wanting to help Mikey's breathing situation, the burn doctors made an appointment with a throat and tracheal specialist about a year after his initial burn.

Dear Reader: How would you like it if you met your surgeon for the first time and discovered his name was Doctor Butcher? I know that sounds like an author's joke, but it is the absolute truth.

He inserted a tiny tube into Mikey's nostril to gain access to the air passage. As with the other physicians who had looked down his throat, albeit without the sophisticated instruments available to Dr. Butcher, he found as they had that the passage was completely blocked. The scars caused by the burns and the intubation tubes passed into his throat during the early days of the ordeal had fused together as one big piece of flesh, allowing no air to pass through. Dr. Butcher, being a surgeon, suggested we operate. He suggested removing one of Mikey's vocal cords and all the scar tissue in order to create a path through which the air to move.

I thought, *If they remove his vocal cord, he'll never be able to speak again.* Although now he could only whisper, yet he still had a small breathy voice if he put his finger over the hole in his throat. I simply could not imagine life without his being able to speak.

Dr. Butcher read my thoughts and said, "I will build him a voice box; he can hold a small microphone to his throat, and learn to speak with that instrument." If you have ever heard people speak with one of these tools used for people who have had their vocal cords removed because of throat cancer, you know it sounds a bit like the *Star Wars* character R2D2.

Mikey placed his finger over the tracheostomy hole, and said in a soft raspy voice, "Doc, you go ahead and remove my vocal cords, 'cause when I get big, God has called me to preach, and I'm gonna preach with or without vocal cords."

What a statement of faith coming from an eight-year-old child! Completely believing that he would speak with or without the assistance of vocal cords!

The next morning, the day before the scheduled surgery, I took Mikey to the New Orleans Audubon Zoo. We strolled through the park chatting, humming, laughing, and watching all the animals staring back at us. The hot breeze blew slightly through thick, low-hanging hundred-year-old oak trees. A dank smell of barnyard and hay lingered in the humid air. The monkeys swung from limb to limb in their cages atop Monkey Hill, having no care in the world. I don't remember how much of the fifty-eight acres of the unique wildlife haven laced with the true New Orleans flavor we walked, but we saw tigers, bears, elephants, elk, snakes, crocodiles, and much more. Much of this zoo dates from the early 20th century. Inside the zoo, we strolled through a real swamp, right in the middle of uptown New Orleans. A Cajun houseboat was on a lagoon full of fourteen-foot alligators. All was beautiful in its own mossy way.

Occasionally we sat on a park bench, not acknowledging in our discussion *the elephant in the room* that was obviously on both our minds and hearts.

What would tomorrow hold? Neither of us had a clue what the next day or the future would unfurl, but we put forth our best effort to enjoy this day given to us by the mercies of God. We praised God for His creation, for the air we breathed, and life. He who holds the tomorrows in His hand is able to keep what we commit to Him. I had an assurance in my heart that somehow, someway, it would all eventually be okay.

Returning across the Lake Ponchartrain causeway to our home in Covington, God filled my heart with a song of victory. I sang loudly of the power of God to deliver. The newly created melody, the word, and the message of the song poured out of my heart and spirit like a river flowing out of its banks. I sang until Mikey put his finger over his trach, and requested I stop for a while.

The next morning, Mikey was wheeled through the double doors into the surgery ward, once again at Ochsner Hospital, only now he was eight, and the sign above the doors read: no entry, stop, do not pass go—that is, for everyone except the surgical staff. We were led away to yet another waiting room where we had to administer great constraint on the battleground of our minds.

That day, Dr. Butcher removed Mikey's vocal cord, thinking this would create a breathing passage for him. Mikey's airway was fused together all the way down his throat. When the fireball exploded like a shooting rocket heading straight for his face, in shock, he had opened his mouth and sucked in the hot flaming air. The fire proceeded down his throat and into his lungs, which accounted for the soot that often clogged the suction tube we used to clear the mucus from his lungs. On the inside, his lungs had been charred as badly as his body had been on the outside.

The ramifications of having his vocal cords surgically removed placed a new pressure on Mike and me for Mikey's personal care. Now he could not speak or even whisper to say, "I cannot breathe"; therefore, our responsibility had instantly increased megafold. I wanted to say to the doctors, "We cannot take him home. What if he stops breathing? What if his trach stops up and he suffocates to death?" However, no one listened to our fears and concerns.

We took him home with great apprehension and trepidation—much like the first time we had brought him home from Shriners. This time was different—more severe in many ways. Before, he could talk in a gravelly whisper to us; however, this time around, he could make NO SOUND AT ALL. His trach stopped up many times a day and throughout the night. The only way he had to get our attention was to clap his hands together. When we managed to fall asleep at night, he clapped loudly and we jumped out of bed, ran to his bedside, and changed his trach so that he could breathe once again.

One of the conditions making this particular time stressful was my family's long generational history of allergies; and Mikey had inherited them all, causing his trach to clog up often day and night. Just the thought of knowing we were responsible for his very breath was emotionally overwhelming. There was no one else to look toward. We had to keep the trachs boiled; we had to keep them changed; we had to keep his lungs suctioned; and there was no way for him to tell us that he was in trouble except clapping his hands together.

The positive aspect of caring for him at home was that Melissa, our daughter, was able to move back into her bedroom. Often she seemed lost in the shuffle during the first year of Mikey's burn.

When staying with one of her best friends, she slept on a pallet on the floor near her friend's pet rabbit's cage. I know these days, weeks, and months were a personal nightmare for her to be separated from her mom, dad, and critically ill brother. We felt we had to shield her from the trauma of his suffering. They say hindsight is 20/20. I'm sure we could have done many things differently, but it's hard not to focus on a child you might not have in days to come. Had the tables been reversed, we would have done the same for her.

Three weeks after the surgery, Mikey and I returned to Dr. Butcher for a post-surgery follow-up. The next plan of action was to make him a voice box for which he would hold up a small amplified microphone at his throat, and it would pick up the sounds resembling the sound of a robot trying to talk.

The doctor eased the tiny tube with a micro-camera on the end through one of his nasal passages. Dr. Butcher could view the area in Mikey's throat where his skilled hands had removed his vocal cord.

He turned to me and said, "Mrs. Cheshier, come take a look at this."

I got up from my seat and walked over to the small screen he was peering at.

"What do you see?" he asked.

All through high school and in college, I studied music. In those classes from time to time we studied the vocal anatomy. The vocal folds, also known as vocal cords, are located within the larynx—also known as the voice box—at the top of the trachea. They are open during inhalation, and come together to close during swallowing and phonation. When closed, the vocal folds may vibrate and modulate the expelled airflow from the lungs to produce speech and singing. The larynx itself consists of two glistening white vocal folds, which form a V-shaped structure. When in use, it can remind you of a butterfly opening and closing its wings. The airway is between the vocal folds.

I said, "Dr. Butcher, it looks to me like butterfly wings—vocal cords—but I know you removed them."

He said, "I never know what to expect from this boy. I cut out his vocal cord with my very own hand; and yes, you see it right. He has a working set of vocal cords. It is a miracle."

At first, I was speechless; then I recalled Mikey's words, "You can have my vocal cords, Doc, 'cause when I get big, I will preach with or without them."

Dr. Butcher proceeded with his explanation, "When you remove a vocal cord, it's an organ—it's like removing an arm or a leg: you don't grow it back. We removed this vocal cord—this organ— and yet, it is there. That's why I say we are looking at a miracle—you don't grow it back—it has miraculously been placed there."

We realized that once again, God had worked a mighty, creative miracle for Mikey. God must have an incredible mission for him to accomplish. What an awesome God we serve. A God who knows no boundaries! A God who can do anything! A God who delights in doing the impossible for us!

This miracle was one of so many now surrounding Mikey's very existence. He was quickly becoming a living testimony of miraculous divine interventions that were almost unbelievable for the natural person; but he was living proof of God's power. Mikey was developing a relationship with God that most people—even Christian people—would never experience. Some people live their entire life and never know the miraculous powers of God. Mikey was living an unbelievable story of his deliverance from the fiery furnace. We were all learning that despite how things look on the outside, God had it under control. He held the entire family in the palm of His mighty hands. He was still ruling and reigning in our hearts.

MIKEY

It's difficult to explain what it's like to simultaneously be both touched by God and disappointed, but this was my predicament upon inspecting the visage in the mirror before me. I *FELT* God's power touch me, and I had hoped it spelled freedom from the scars and pain. However, in reality, it was something different, but just as miraculous. In short order, that morning after being prayed for, we went home from church, and I found myself staring into the looking glass. Hair had punched through all the scar tissue on my scalp, creating a full head covering. It was a miracle, no doubt—one many hair-challenged men might hope for. However, for me, it was disappointing that God did not decide to repair what I thought important, and, still yet, He poured out a power to trump and alter the physical law.

Concerning God's sovereignty, I have had to learn this one time-tested truth, and trust it time and time again throughout my journey with Jesus. We have an *idea* in our heads how we think things ought to go; and so we let God in on the information, and then expect Him to step in and do our bidding—working out our schemes and plans. Here was an occasion where I, like the man at the pool in Scripture, went to the altar in hopes of the Spirit moving through that place, and brushing His wing of favor against my body as He passed by. I brought a desire for effect to my Savior—nothing short of removing my scars and suffering. I came and was joined by His children, coupling their prayer with mine. We were poised for God to do our bidding and move on our desires. Now, here was the moment when God visited us, heard us, and applied His power to grow hair through melted follicles—impossible, astounding, stunning, and praiseworthy, yet not at all the focus of our faith. How frustrating for Him to dangle His power in front of us, only to deny my focus of hope. Removing the evidence of my catastrophe was what I thought, in my scope of knowledge, to be ideal in my situation; however, the Creator of the universe disagreed.

I know many will read this book and wonder why God has not moved on your behalf.

Today I carry scars and pain that He could have altered at that moment, had He seen it as useful to the greater plan, yet He did not deem it best. Therein is the truth God brought to clarity in me, and it has developed a trust relationship that is unshakable. He has a plan. The plan is His— taking into consideration the length and breadth of all your life in regard to each movement He makes on your behalf along the way, and each time your requests are denied. It is not as if He is in heaven denying your requests and saying, "Oh,

I'll show them who is boss." No, may it never be. Rather, God would say, "Oh, child, you wouldn't make such requests if you simply could see what I see; you would know it isn't best for you." How can the creation disparage against Creator concerning these things? The Scriptures make it clear that God does "good" to those who serve and love Him. This being the case, I must agree that what He does for me is good, and what He does not do for me is good also. Let that sink in a moment. I can look back now with joy for His denial of full healing in that moment; the reason will become clear to the reader in time through this story.

MARIGOLD

One particular Sunday evening, about two years after his burn, we had an incredible move of God's Spirit at our church where we pastored on the north shore of Lake Ponchartrain. Mikey came to the platform for prayer. When prayed over, he was slain in the Spirit for a long period of time—some thirty to forty minutes. When he got to his feet he said, "Mom take my Jobst garments off; I believe the Lord has healed me." I unfastened the Velcro strip that held the Jobst tightly in place. The Jobst held a mask to his charred, scarred face. Both of our expectations were high when he leaned forward and allowed the face mask to fall in his hand after the Jobst had been taken away. He looked at me for my reaction. His face still bore the scars—the hot red angry scars of his burn. He really thought that God had removed all of his scars from the burn. It made my heart sad to see his let-down.

Disappointed, he turned to walk away. As he turned to leave, I said, "Mikey wait up, you did have a miracle."

On the back of his head had been a burned place in his scalp larger than a half dollar almost the size of a canning jar lid. The doctors said no hair would ever grow there; but miraculously that place was covered with hair—the burned place on his head had been just as hot and red and raised as all the other burn scars!

Truly, we had seen another miracle right before our very eyes. Why did God not just remove his burn scars? Why did he have to be burned in the first place? Why did his lungs and throat have to be burned together? To these questions, I will never know the answers this side of heaven. The same God that gave him a working set of vocal cords could have prevented the entire incident. The same God that healed the scar in his scalp could have healed the scars on his face.

To the why questions, we'll never have an answer until we stand before God. Perhaps we will think to ask Him about some of the trials of life, but then it won't matter a whit. The important thing is that we trust Him. The important thing is not that He works the miracle we want Him to work, but that He has His way, and we trust His way even though we cannot see the immediate reason. He sees the whole picture, whereas we only see what we experience. This is where the real battle comes in—the battle for the mind.

I remember a time not too long after the original crisis with Mikey when we were visiting some dear friends on the bayou in Lacombe, Louisiana. Mike noticed a wall hanger with a beautiful truth embroidered on cloth in a frame. It said something to the effect that life is like a tapestry. We can only see the underneath side which has a confusing tangle of multi-colored threads seemingly hanging in disarray without purpose, but the master artist sees the top, which when we see it in eternity will show our lives as a beautiful work of art.

**That, Dear Reader, is what TRUST is all about. The battlefield of the mind where the sword swings back-and-forth with the why questions, and with how it could have turned out so differently—and the sword goes back-and-forth. This is the real battle: deciding what we will

*do with what has been handed us in life, and how
we will respond to a crisis. We cannot waste our
time entertaining a blame game, a game of
accusing, a game of questioning. We must guard
our mind at all times and bring it into subjection,
or this will be the avenue the enemy uses to
destroy us. We must never forget that a continual
war—a battle for our souls—is being fought in the
heavens over every single one of us. It is not what
happens to us that destroys us. However, our
response to happenings in our lives can destroy
us.*

MIKEY

This marked the first miracle after my release
from the hospital. Many more followed—some we
do not know when they were made, and some
that marked monuments of triumph in my history
with walking with my Redeemer.

The days followed in a cycle of sorts: I had some
occasions of terrible fear and despair; I lamented
and trembled; but God reminded of His goodness
and humbled me; then in humility, I committed to
Him my suffering, and He answered with wisdom
and authority. I imagine that if I tried, I could find
some crisis in either my body or my mind for each
daily breath to take up pages of this accounting.

The war and suffering were relentless without an option of finding a moment to catch my breath—once one fire was put out (pun intended), another blazed up demanding full force to try and contain it. This was every day—not just Mondays, but every day. You might think I am being dramatic at this juncture, trying to elicit some response of sympathy from you; this is not so, I seek only to be honest. The physicality of this suffering was attached to trying to talk, trying to breathe, trying to move, and trying to get comfortable—all daily achievements. Couple with this the mental and emotional war raging within me. The aspect of being uneasy and ashamed every time eyes fell upon me; each word spoken being filtered through expectation of response to my disfigurement; the obvious aspect of being isolated and unique in an age group and culture which strives to group oneself with like persons for empowerment and courage. Each day of life was an embodiment of suffering on physical and metaphysical fronts. I do not wish to take the reader through each and every day because, chiefly, I don't want anyone to have to live the experiences I was allotted each day. Secondly, and more relative to the issue I now face, is expedience. It would take too long to itemize each moment of trouble; and, frankly, I don't want to subject myself to recollection of the sheer volume of pain experienced. Let this then satisfy questions for specifics: the moments of despair and doubt were as numerous as the interactions I had for the years that followed my moment of combustion.

My family settled into a mode of forward progress—not to say normalcy because life was furthest from that. I had to try to adapt to what was going on, and move forward with normal things, while not at all being as such myself. For instance, I desperately desired to go to school— public school at that. To be honest, I think it was the need for commonality with others that drove me to want to be a part.

I attended public school one hour a day during the third grade. My real teaching took place at home. I was burned in the middle of the second grade; however, I had a fifth grade reading comprehension, which helped me to stay ahead of the game, and not to lose grade advancement. During the third grade I advanced to ninth grade reading comprehension. When they tested my IQ at Shriners Burn Hospital, it was discovered that I tested with a genius IQ. God is good.

To attend public school, my mom had to be in close attendance throughout the day. She made a tremendous sacrifice to be at the school, particularly in those early months, to maintain my wounds and the breathing apparatus in my neck.

Those things became a constant source of ridicule from other children around me. They made fun of me incessantly for being different. However different I was, it was some measure of comfort to do something other children my age did. Just some piece of being like others was so inviting.

Since the tracheotomy in my neck lasted for nearly seven years after the fact of my burn, these challenges extended for many years of schooling, creating unique challenges and opportunities. As I look back in time to these moments—however hurtful and however dark—I am reminded that I am the sum total of all variables and experiences. I would not be who I am today as I stand with experiences and insights that can only be born out of suffering, had I not suffered as I did. There is a value ascribed to all this since the Lord has redeemed the horror to blessing—and that cannot be cheapened! Oftentimes when I think of milestones in my past, it isn't when I walked the stage at graduation, or my first swim, or anything as mundane as the experience of every other person. My recollections of milestones in the past are more comparable to the day my tracheotomy came out, or the day I led my first person to Jesus, or the first miracle I saw, or the day my dad had to put his knee on my chest and shove the tracheotomy back into a hole that had rapidly closed . . . good times.

The list of ailments I had interjected itself at nearly every turn. At first, I could hardly communicate in real time because I had no voice. To communicate in school and with classmates was challenging. My teachers bore a frustration for their learning environment constantly being interrupted by the distractions as I left class to get medical care and need to go to the restroom to address one issue or another. We have a tendency to just say, "Hey, he has an issue; show some grace"; but in reality, I expected the whole world to bend, allowing me a chance for this or that. It was somewhat unfair to all those who hadn't make the monumental error of setting themselves on fire. Often times we get so myopic in our situation, we fail to look beyond our own suffering to see its effect on those around us.

My burn did not simply have implications for me, but for every soul that decided to be or was required to be a part of my life. My friends had to assume a responsibility of attention if they wanted to be near me. As an example, at personal expense, a precious Catholic girl determined to show me kindness by sitting next to me on the bus I rode home from school. I recall hundreds of times when I came into the focused crosshairs of horrible human response. Words were directed at me to cut and hurt only because I was different. Others were unaccustomed and even made uncomfortable by my differences. Many times I felt as though by my disturbing the happy facade that everything is always sunshine and rainbows, people resented me. I remember children saying, "We wished you would have died so we don't have to look at you."

It was a constant in my life. It got to the point that I rarely, if ever, confessed these things to family because, number one, it was frustrating as they could do little to nothing to amend the situation, and, secondly, because I wasn't always sure they believed the level of hell I experienced at the hands of children's torment. It was my burden to bear, and my fault for being here; so it was mostly something I brought to Jesus. The interesting thing was, I understood. I was not so ignorant as to sit in a seat and say, "Why are you treating me this way?" On the contrary, I was in a position of saying, "I am sorry that you are to be subjected to me and my suffering." It was not until college that I became completely comfortable in being in an organized institution, mainly because by that time most humans had come into a measure of suffering to be sympathetic to a fellow man who simply had it a little worse at moments.

The support and care of my family was a constant uplift to the horrible and cruel world outside the walls of my home. I deeply understand the idea of refuge. My home was a refuge, a place of love and care and more or less normal treatment. My parents became a driving force in returning their boy to functionality. I will say this: they never tolerated anything in me considered to be weakness or self-loathing. They pointed to wellness and continuously pressed me in that direction. Aided by the fact I didn't want to be any less than well, I refused to let them park in handicap spaces, did as much of my treatment as I could, and wanted to be a part of things normal people did. This sentiment was fine and good but hindered by realities—one being, the lack of movement to full extension of my arms. My father took this ailment under his supervision. He pressed me to be vigilant in working out this area. I stretched against the protest of the damaged skin, which felt like bringing my arms to the edge of tearing the flesh that seemed so insistent on being confined. He also bought me a pellet gun, and took me out to shoot at a nearby river. Pumping the gun required that I stretch against the pull of the skin. I recall many times, his bringing me out for this kind of therapy, which turned out to be a fantastic bonding period with my father. He was determined not to lose his son—not to fire and not to depression, or any similar self-inflicted malady.

For the purposes of this testimony, you must understand that except for my respiratory system, my physical person healed within a few months of departure from the hospital. The respiratory aspect of my wounds hung on for years—my tracheotomy maintained its grip for nearly seven years after my initial burn. Breathing wise and vocally, I still bear difficulties and issues from the occurrence. Not to say I am on some level non-functional. I truly attack and do what very healthy people refuse to do as I head out yearly in exploratory missions work where we sleep in tents, and pack in our food and water. However, the evidence of my outward damages—signaled by poor vocal quality and heavier breathing—are embodied within the scars and the inward damages.

There are three major moments I want to communicate in my Lord's complex process of bringing about healing for me internally.

First, my tracheotomy, as I said, held on for years. This was not because we sat idly by and allowed it to be so. Having a trach is a very risky prospect in terms of illness and longevity. God, in His wisdom, placed many checks and balances in the respiratory system between the mouth and the lungs. What the trach accomplishes is bypassing these filters and safeties. Everything in the air—viruses, smoke, moisture, and the like—has a clear shot into your lungs, and can very easily compromise wellbeing. Not to mention, as this was my sole source to breath, and it was easily blocked, I was regularly under a threat of suffocation. As a result, it was a priority to see this apparatus removed. The problem was my tendency to scar badly. After initial revelations that my throat was webbed shut, surgeries were attempted, and scar tissue impeded progress.

One surgery among dozens conducted for this condition was to cut out my vocal cords. I was eight years old. My doctor felt as though this was a fair trade—a permanent loss of voice for freedom from the trach. We decided to follow his lead, but in the pre-surgery visits, I told him very clearly in a raspy, broken voice without speech delivery cadence, "With or without vocal cords I am going to preach." He looked at me with great pity and sympathy, realizing the foolish sentiment of a child, and lack of understanding for the way things really are.

The surgery was conducted and I was sent home; my vocal cords were removed. Two weeks passed and I began to make noise. We scheduled an appointment to see what was happening as this was literally a physical impossibility. I can tell you this: I was so fixated on God doing something amazing that I was not surprised. I had a sense in my very soul causing me to confess that I would preach regardless. Jesus was planning something great! When we arrived at the office, the doctor took a long, skinny tube with a camera on the end of it, and inserted it into my nose to look in my throat. I always thought that was weird when seemingly my mouth was a much more convenient access point to arrive at his desired destination . . . I digress.

He looked into the scope and then leaned back with a wide-eyed look as if he had beheld a specter. He spoke, "Mrs. Cheshier, can you look into the scope and tell me what you see?"

She retorted as she leaned into the eyepiece, "What am I supposed to see?" Then, "I see two things moving around."

That confession hung in the air for a moment until he spoke softly, "I cut those out two weeks ago."

God had regrown or replaced an organ within my neck! A physical and medical impossibility—yet a trivial gesture of His power extended so that His will be rendered! This was a pivotal moment of both joy and frustration—joy that God was still involved and had a plan, but a frustration that this plan may not involve healing me of my trach.

The doctor would no longer work on me. I can't blame him really, because if what you cut out comes back, that's counterproductive. I also think it freaked him out a little bit.

We decided to look into other means of medical answers for my trach. It might seem there was a lack of faith present if we continued to try to find answers, but in reality, we operated in the knowledge that we had until God made His exact plan clear. It would be a tragedy if God showed a man His intention to miraculously heal him, then the man tried some medical answer instead. However, until God made His will clear, we had to walk in the wisdom He had given, and try to alleviate my suffering. At any rate, we tried several other options. One such unsuccessful option when I was nine years old was to remove cartilage from my jaw, and implant it in my neck. Many attempts were made to laser cut sections of webbing and scar tissue from my neck, all to no avail.

When I was eleven, the last such surgery on my throat took part of my rib and stinted it in my neck, along with some laser cuts that would hopefully heal with the aid of being held apart by the rib. This apparatus was wired in my throat with barbs coming out of either side of my neck. Imagine the silver trach tied with one-half inch cotton ribbon squarely embedded in my throat, and then two surgical wires protruding out in a Frankenstein-esque manner. I was a sight to behold! The g'day oddity of my appearance that had plagued my life was only compounded by the new additions. It was a lonely and low time of hopeful healing.

One night at church just before my fourteenth birthday, I felt a pop in my neck—the unthinkable had happened—the wire had broken and the rib went long-ways in my air canal. I was dying again. Having to make a seven- or eight-hour journey in a RV to the hospital that had done the procedure intensified the sheer terror of this moment. Every instant seemed as though the rib would position just so, and I would breathe my last breath. We took the RV, not a plane or ambulance, because it was the smoother ride, and any jarring could spell disaster. Upon arriving at the hospital, I was rushed into surgery where they removed the apparatus, and subsequently delivered the troubling news. "We have done all we can for you. This trach will be there for the rest of your life."

In that profound moment, like the woman with the issue of blood, I remembered a long road of struggle to only arrive at defeat.

It was there in that state I felt the presence of God overwhelm my person, and His power shook my insides. I felt heat and intensity in my person and was driven to make a confession. "I am healed!" I said out loud.

The doctor did his best to be patient, and assumed I had not been listening to all the perfectly logical, medical reasons as to why I was not healed.

I said, "Let me do the breathing test again."

He was kind enough to oblige me, even though his certainty of similarly failed results was imminent. Something wonderful transpired: I breathed as I never had before, and it came easy and strong.

The doctor immediately took his scope and looked into my throat. After peering into the eyepiece, he leaned back as if he had seen a specter, only this time he smiled. Taking a pair of scissors, they cut the cotton strap that had held my only source of life in place for six years. They took hold of my tracheotomy, and began to pull it out. I felt the drag of the cool metal one last time sliding from the skin in my neck. I saw the smiles. I could hardly believe it. God had done what we, in all our strength and attempts, could not do—He had freed me from my prison of the tracheotomy.

I can't expect you to fully understand the weight of the occurrence here. I would liken it unto this: let us say you were placed into handcuffs for seven years. They were removed only two times or so a day in order to clean them for fear they might cause an infection on your wrist. Where you might expect to have joy at their removal, what you had instead was a trembling and trepidation that you would die without them, and you needed them replaced as soon as possible.

For more than six years—since I was seven years old—now I was thirteen years old—I had been in bondage, attached by invisible cords to humidifiers and suction machines and boiling water to clean. Freedom was not available to me, but it was needed, and I feared what would happen if I was granted freedom from requiring the trach. God alleviated all my fear and bondage in that moment. By His very divine power, the impossible was done!

MARIGOLD

Seven years later, we accepted the pastorate in Perrysburg, Ohio, the last pastorate in which we would try to balance missions evangelism and pastoring. Mike told the board that we would give them five years, then we would go into missions full time. He asked if we could continue our missions work every three months, and the board agreed. The first Sunday we were there, the church gave a reception to welcome our coming. Mikey still wore the stainless steel trach with the ties holding it in place. During the reception he began to notice real breathing problems. The problem continued to escalate until we felt like we needed to take him to a hospital; however, his condition was so complex, we felt it necessary to get him to St. Jude in St. Louis, nine hours away. Albert Lentz, part of our new church family, had come to the celebration in their lovely large RV. There are many snowbirds in the Toledo area. They love giving their time in ministry to the MAPS program in the Deep South during the hard mid-western winters. They were so kind to drive Mikey to the hospital. A bed was made for him on the couch in the living room, and we all piled into the RV and headed for St. Louis. Mikey hardly moved. Once again I sat on the floor beside him, praying for God to intervene. I thought the trip would never end. I feared he might stop breathing all together. "God please help our little son. Don't let him die in this RV. Be his breath and help us, dear Father," I prayed.

As we pulled into the parking lot at St. Jude, Mikey completely crashed. Every breath seemed his last. The medical crew was waiting at the emergency entrance for him. They whisked him into surgery after just one look at him. Mikey had had three unsuccessful surgeries over the past seven years to set him free from the trach. Even the implant of bone and cartilage two years before—a last ditch effort—had failed. The doctors finally gave up, saying Mikey would wear the trach the remainder of his life on earth.

Several hours later, the surgeon came to the lobby where we were all waiting. "Mr. and Mrs. Cheshier, we have witnessed yet another miracle today. The reason your son's trach was pushing out, cutting off his airway, was because his body was trying to rid itself of the foreign object. His airway is so wide and clear that you could run a Mac truck through it. We have removed the trach tube from his trachea. A hole remains in his neck, but it will gradually close up on its own."

After seven years of breathing through a metal tube harnessed to his neck, Mikey was finally free—an absolutely Divine miracle from our miraculous Lord. Once again God brought deliverance.

MIKEY

A TROPHY TO THE POWER OF GOD

Years passed and many stories are intertwined within those days, most of tremendous God-given victories. I played football and track, and lifted weights . . . I lived.

There is something you should know, though. I want to share a precious memory with you.

We had just completed several weeks of missions work in the East Africa area. We had a little time to spare and decided to go hunting in Tanzania with a friend, Colonel Mongi—as his name suggests, a part of the Tanzanian army. As we drove into Moshi, Tanzania, he received communication that some disturbance required his attention, and we were not going to be able to hunt. Though disheartened, we would not be denied some R&R. Mount Kilimanjaro was nearby. We decided to climb this natural wonder. Making short work of preparation, we began to climb this amazing mountain with our gear and a guide and helper-type folk carrying excess gear. Passing through several layers of different ecosystems, we ascended from one camp to the next. The trip covered several days and more than sixty miles. I spent the first day and more in wide-eyed wonder at the beauty surrounding me, knowing only a minimal portion of the world's population could enjoy it. The last day before our final ascent, I was singing worship songs as we climbed. This accomplishment was becoming a determined trophy—a victory shared by only a select few on the planet—and here I was with my past and present burdens setting one foot in front of another . . . I could not fail here.

We arrived at the last camp about five o'clock in the afternoon where we went in to sleep as able, to prepare for a midnight departure for the summit, our final ascent. I admittedly don't really know if I slept or not. I was thinking about the next day and the challenge it represented. Awakened at 11:30 p.m., we stepped outside to cold, crisp air, whereas it had been hot at times, as we had traveled up the mountainside. The moon was so close I felt as if I could reach out and grab it as it floated there in the crystal blue clear night sky. We set out; this last section was ashy and hard to manage. With labored breathing, it was hard to continue. I had to. On more than one occasion as the night gave way to morning I thought of turning around, but I had to do this . . . no matter the cost. Something had been birthed in my mind, and it would not be set aside. Arriving near the crest, I caught sight of Kili's glacier and her peak. This sight aided my resolve that the trophy was attainable, and so I pressed on step-by-step. At this altitude, my water bottles froze, and I began to throw up as the famed altitude sickness made sport of my equilibrium. I didn't care; nothing could keep me from the peak . . . nothing. With every ounce of my will, I set foot upon her highest point, "Uhuru" Peak, which means "freedom" in the native tongue of Swahili. I fell to my knees—not out of exhaustion, but rather out of humility. There was something I had to do. I didn't care who heard me as I began to pray aloud in front of a handful of other climbers and my guide. "Father, I have never had anything to give You in return for what You have done . . . nothing. You have made good out of all the messes I have made of my life. In this moment, at this place, I make an offering. Here, Lord, is the evidence of Your mastery, Your greatness, Your provision, Your love, and I offer You this: my greatest physical achievement in honor of You making it possible." I laid down my trophy of reaching "Freedom" Peak; after all, it wasn't mine anyway.

Everything I am and have was purchased by the blood of Jesus and the mercy of our Father. I am a physical representation of supernatural intervention.

MARIGOLD

Today our son is a husband, father, evangelist, pastor, missionary trailblazer, and defender of the cause of Jesus Christ. To God be all the glory.

9

EPILOGUE

By Mike Cheshier

What you have just read from Marigold and Mikey, with some editorializing from me, has been one of the most soul-grinding, gut-wrenching projects of our lives, other than living the experiences in the present tense some thirty-three years ago. We have not shared these things for sympathy, nor to receive any accolades for bravery, or to put ourselves forward as examples of mighty warriors for God. I can tell you we all agree that while we would not take anything for lessons learned about our Father in the fire, we are glad to be out of the crucible and would not want to live another second of those events.

Even the telling of the story was most difficult for all of us, but most of all for Mikey. I recall on one occasion that Marigold wanted Mikey to carefully peruse something he wrote. He simply told her to fix it as needed because as he ruminated on those things he could literally smell his charred flesh, and actually feel the pain of some of the procedures that he had to endure. Our goal is to prayerfully offer hope to some of our fellow travelers on this "Road of the Pilgrim" to the Promised Land, that there IS a city whose Builder and Maker is God, and it is worth any sacrifices on the journey, and you, too, can make it no matter what you are facing.

I must at this moment offer credit to most of the "body of Christ" at this point as we owe more than we can ever repay to so many members of said body who are heroes in this battle we fought. I remember so well the day I was pacing the hall of OchsnerHospital when the Lutheran pastor from our town entered that hall, walked up to me, and stated he had a word from God for us. Now, as I jokingly say, that surprised me because I didn't know God spoke to Lutherans. However, at that time the doctors were telling us that our son would probably not live through this, and we needed to hear from the Father from any source. Ray proceeded to read to me the 27th Psalm and came to the verse where it says, *"You shall see the [mercy] of the Lord in the land of the living."* After reading that passage, he and his wife joined hands with Marigold and me in the busy hall of that great hospital with people walking on both sides of us, and began to pray in the Holy Ghost!!!! As the old timers used to describe the experience, I could have had a "Holy Ghost Seizure" right there in that busy hall. I knew our son was going to live because I had the Lord's word on it and from a faithful, Spirit-led Brother!!

I would not fail to mention because we needed to be with our son nearly 24/7 that a well-known pastor, Brother Marvin Gorman, paid for us to stay in the guest quarters of the hospital rather than drive the nearly forty miles back home each evening. I will also never forget that the leader of the biggest television ministry in the world at that time took the time to call our son because someone from that work visited Mikey, and he told his visitor to have "Brother Jimmy" to call him. Can you imagine our surprise when this man interrupted his incredibly busy schedule and did so!!! There were so many more nondescript believers who prayed hours for Mikey, and many who gave to help alleviate the crushing financial burden incurred. Our Heroes, all of them! All the members of our family are included, especially Mikey's sister, Melissa, who endured neglect and isolation because we did not know for so long whether Mikey would make it or not. All are heroes.

On the flip side of this, there were those whom we knew well who attempted to add to our pain by placing their theology above mercy by telling us that had we known our "power of authority" (whatever that means), our son would not have been burned. The man who told this to our people we were pastoring was a leading television personality with whom I was well acquainted, and he never once called to tell us he was praying for us. If you know someone who is going through the fire, put theology aside and ENCOURAGE HIM!!!!

If you, at this time in your life are facing something you do not understand, let me give you a word of encouragement. You CAN get through it if you will follow these simple steps.

FORGET THE *"WHY"* QUESTION!!!! There may be no answer until we get to heaven. Then it won't matter. That is what TRUST is all about.

RUN TO THE WORD!!!! My word was 1 Corinthians 10:13 NIV paraphrased: *"There has no test taken you but such as is common to man, but God who is faithful will with that test make a way of escape, and you shall not be tested above that which you are able to bear."*

Believe me, there were times when I told God He had more confidence in me than I did. But here we are, blessed beyond measure, and all of our family is in the ministry.

The other word came from the passage set in the time where Jesus fed the 5,000, and then began to speak in spiritual terms, and the Bible says His disciples stopped following Him because He was feeding them spiritually and not literally. He turned to the Twelve and asked, " 'Will *you also go away?' Peter answered for me when he said, 'Lord to whom shall we go? You have the words of eternal life.' "*

Whatever you do, don't forsake your own mercy.

FOCUS ON THE CROSS!!!! You cannot look at the cross and see what Jesus went through, and feel sorry for yourself.

The great Christian writer, C. S. Lewis, wrote a wonderful thesis called, "The Problem of Pain" in which he shared concerning the death of his wife—the "love of his life"—whom he married late in life. His basic principle was: there is pain in life, but HIS GRACE IS SUFFICIENT. THAT is exactly what Marigold and Mikey are saying, "HIS GRACE IS SUFFICIENT."

All the other stories are more of the "Chronicles of the Call." We sincerely hope you enjoy all these offerings from what I consider one of the finest "storytellers" you will ever read. Marigold will once again have you laughing and crying from one line to the next. Her second grade school teacher once said because of her wonderful imagination she would one day be a great writer. I believe she was speaking prophetically.

Mike and Marigold Cheshier

ENDNOTES

[1]Because He Lives, William J. Gaither & Gloria Gaither EP292240 (1971).

In the story "Chains, Quagmires, and Night Stalkers," the night was black. Therefore, we could not take pictures of the animals pacing around our vehicle. On another occasion in the same area, this cheetah tried his best to climb into our vehicle. Though it was late in the evening, we had enough light to snap this shot.

"God Sent a Warthog"

"God Sent a Warthog"

"Monkey Business"

"Monkey Business"

249

Max McGough in "Nosing Around"

One of the roads described in "Of Mud and Ministry"

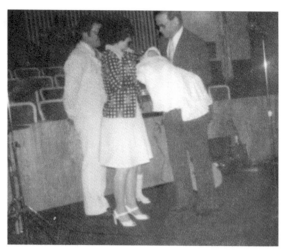

Mikey was dedicated to the Lord in March, 1975
by my dad, J. E. Allen

Mikey, age 2½

Shortly before Mikey's burn in the winter of 1982

Mikey was part of the "Living Witnesses"
Easter Cantata, 1985

Our family in 1988

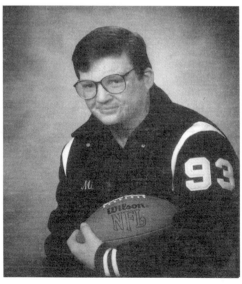

Mikey was part of the high school football team, 1993

Mikey, his wife Shereen and children,
Serenity and Gabriel

Our daughter, Melissa, her husband, Adam,
and sons, Maurice and Michael